7 Easy Steps to Safe and Fun Boarding

NO-FALL

SNOWBOARDING

by
Danny Martin

with Matt Diehl

photographs by Mark Seliger

A FIRESIDE BOOK
Published by Simon & Schuster
New York   London   Toronto   Sydney

FIRESIDE
Rockefeller Center
1230 Avenue of the Americas
New York, NY 10020

Copyright © 2005 by Danny Martin
Photographs by Mark Seliger
All rights reserved,
including the right of reproduction
in whole or in part in any form.

FIRESIDE and colophon are registered trademarks
of Simon & Schuster, Inc.

Designed by Jaime Putorti

For information regarding special discounts for bulk purchases,
please contact Simon & Schuster Special Sales at
1-800-456-6798 or business@simonandschuster.com

Manufactured in the United States of America

10   9   8   7   6   5   4   3   2   1

Library of Congress Cataloging-in-Publication Data

Martin, Danny.
    No-fall snowboarding / by Danny Martin, with Matt Diehl.
        p.   cm.
1. Snowboarding.   I. Diehl, Matt.   II. Title.
GV857.S57M3526   2005
796.93'9—dc22   2005051603

ISBN-13: 978-0-7432-6990-2
ISBN-10   0-7432-6990-X

For my mother

Danny Martin

For my father, Lawrence Diehl, my literary "uncles," John Reque and Anthony DeCurtis, and of course my mother, Carol Diehl. I hold all of you responsible . . .

Matt Diehl

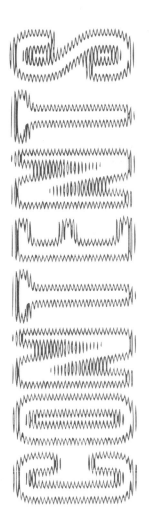

Danny Martin Demystifies the Top Ten Myths About Learning to Snowboard. Dude . . .

1. "You're not learning if you're not falling." (*False.*)
2. "Just have faith—the board will come around." (*And hit you on the head!*)
3. "You have to look in the direction you want to go." (*Snowboard correctly, and you can look wherever you like—or need to.*)
4. "Snowboarders aren't nice. (*Hey, I'm nice.*)
5. "Steering with your lower body is the only way to turn." (*Wrong!*)
6. "Your instructor spends more time snowboarding than you do." (*Not bloody likely.*)
7. "I'm too old to learn to snowboard." (*Actually one of my oldest—and best—students was in his late eighties.*)
8. "Skiers are way cooler than snowboarders." (*Sure they are.*)
9. "Snowboarding's not as fun as skiing." (*Wrong again—it's more fun.*)
10. "You're not learning if you're not falling." (*This one's so damaging, it bears repeating—falling doesn't teach you anything.*)

NO-FALL

SNOWBOARDING

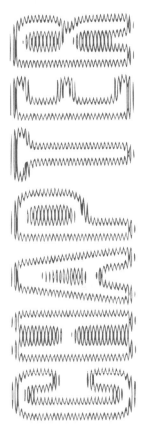

Step 1—Open Your Mind

Snowboarding Is Pain—and Other Lies

> People, no matter how much you
> show them how to balance, will still
> be disproportionately afraid of falling.
> —Dr. Roger Callahan,
> PSYCHOLOGIST/CO-AUTHOR,
> *Tapping the Healer Within*

Snowboarding is *pain*!"

That, my friend, is a lie. A lie you'll hear a lot. Maybe a lie you've heard before. But don't believe it.

However, those were the first words spoken to a beginning snowboarding class taught by one of my co-workers during my first-ever stint teaching snowboarding, circa 1991. She was right in some sense: snowboarding *is* pain—if you learn it the wrong way. Unfortunately, the wrong way is the way most snowboarding is taught.

Winston Churchill once said, "People stumble over the

truth frequently, but most just pick themselves up and carry on as if nothing happened." I never fully accepted the inevitability of falling while attached to a snowboard. I saw my colleague's declaration that "snowboarding is pain" at the beginning of that class as her way of throwing down of the gauntlet.

In effect, she was saying that those who choose to keep falling are tough enough to join the elite ranks of snowboarders, those proudly fearless and feared shredders of the mountain. "Are you tough enough to tough it out?" was the underlying implication.

If snowboarding is pain, well, even the toughest can't take it when taught the wrong way. Eddie Graham is a man who knows his way around serious athletic behavior: he's a noted personal trainer and former wrestler with several New York City Marathons under his belt. But he couldn't handle learning to snowboard. "I was up in Vermont, and a well-meaning surfer friend from California tried to teach me snowboarding," Graham recalls. "I fell so much I just didn't pursue it." Graham's disastrous lesson only got worse as it wore on: "I wound up falling so much that I ended up renting skis for the rest of the day."

Snowboarding incorrectly can indeed fell the mighty like they've never been taken down before. Some years ago, while on staff at a well-known winter resort I encountered a medical crew attending to one of America's most famous athletes. He was bleeding from the head.

This well-known football player was, in fact, famous most of all for being tough: thanks to his daunting speed and size, his crushing tackle is notorious. That he had nearly as many Super Bowl rings as fingers was ample confirmation of his badass reputation.

Snowboarding proved to be the match for this not-so-gentle giant—at least snowboarding taught incorrectly. Mr. Super Bowl Rings told the paramedics tending to his head wound that, despite all those tackles he'd taken on the gridiron, taking a fall snowboarding was the hardest hit he'd ever taken in his sporting life. This was someone whose job was to run into a line of rabid giants intent on taking him down, and he was felled by just one tumble in the snow. "Hmmmm, maybe snowboarding *is* pain," I thought.

On another occasion, I witnessed one of the most famous financial geniuses in America being brought to his knees by the challenge of bad snowboard instruction. This man, whose name is synonymous with money, and lots of it, transformed how we understand capitalism. Snowboarding the wrong way transformed him into an outpatient.

Seeing all this caused questions to rattle through the recesses of my mind: This man was not just famous—and *very* rich—he was old enough to be worried about the brittleness of his bones. Why wasn't his snowboard instructor more worried about him breaking them?

If the people teaching snowboarding didn't care whether or not their highest-profile clients hurt themselves, I wondered, how much did they care if your average Joe Blow split his skull while spending his precious days of Human Resources–allotted vacation trying to learn? I found a clue in a 2002 study from the National Ski Areas Association: "The sports involve some inherent risk, but in some measure, it is that risk that entices most skiers and riders to pursue the sport."

This statement suggests that the "risk" involved in winter sports is sexy and addictive in the way that, say, gambling is. And there are those who do fit the stereotype: some "extreme" snowboarders routinely risk life and limb for adrenalized fun. But the truth is more typically the opposite. From my teaching experience, I know that most people want to *minimize* risk while riding as much as possible, and experts agree. Joe

Blow *does* care about getting injured at a winter resort, according to Dr. Roger Callahan, clinical psychologist and co-author of *Tapping the Healer Within*. "Fear of falling is especially relevant in the context of snowboarding, skiing—even ice skating," Dr. Callahan says. "I don't find it much anywhere else." No surprise, fear of falling is worry *numero uno* for the beginner snowboarder, who faces a tough enough challenge as it is. But whether you're a novice boarder or an "expert," you can benefit from my no-fall technique.

Who Needs No-Fall Snowboarding

Part of the purpose of this book is to help both those who consider themselves experienced snowboarders and the beginners who *wish* to be snowboarders understand the underlying scientific theory behind my technique as they learn it. That's why, as you'll read in later chapters, I put my technique to the test against not just fitness experts, but a distinguished professor of physics, too. Don't believe me—believe *them*. Or you can ask my satisfied clients.

Ever since I invented no-fall snowboarding, my career has boomed, thanks to word-of-mouth recommendations from satisfied customers. I now travel the world snowboarding, from Europe and South America to Australia and Africa, making much more than I ever did as a resort-staff instructor. And as I continue teaching snowboarding, money has become less important. Better snowboarding instruction will make the world a better place, and help the sport grow even more.

Parents definitely need to consider safety when their kids want to take up snowboarding. Do you really want your child stuck with a screwed-up wrist for the rest of her life because her first instructor didn't have her best interests at heart? But snowboarding's not just for grommets anymore. While the sport has a wild, youthful image, it continues to grow not just across gender gaps, but generations.

In snowboarding, age ain't nothin' but a number. Of the nearly 4 million and counting U.S. citizens who consider themselves snowboarders, the biggest demographic growth area is adults thirty years old and over and kids twelve years old and younger (*IDEA Personal Trainer*, October 2000). The oldest student I've ever had, Banana George, was in his mid-eighties: after just a few lessons he was tearing up the mountain like a teenager! At the other end of the spectrum is one of today's top pro snowboarders, Shaun White. As a little kid, Shaun was such a good rider he entered the pro circuit at just thirteen years old—and is just barely college age today.

Many such students are former longtime skiers. It's not easy to teach a middle-aged ski dog new tricks: even though they've skied their entire lives, this group can't return to the poles and sticks once they've tasted the freedom of boarding. Even seasoned snowboarders, the ones that "know it all," can learn from my technique, too. Snowboarders are creatures of habit. It's not unusual to find even a highly decorated snowboarding pro riding with a strange, unorthodox, awkward stance of his or her own devising. If that's the way he or she got used to riding, they're unlikely to change, even if there's a more effective way.

First-Snowboard-Lesson Hell: Sound Familiar?

Then there's those who took one disastrous snowboard lesson and never went back. Does that sound familiar? One student of mine, a writer, never wanted to snowboard again after his first group lesson. For one, he didn't receive much individual attention: his instructor, an amiably stoned twentysomething, seemed overwhelmed by trying to teach fifteen students at one time, preferring instead to flirt with a couple of cute Brazilian girls.

The writer's first tumble came at the chair lift: Mr. Amiably Stoned never bothered to explain how to get on and off the darn thing. And when the writer tried to snowboard down what seemed a scarifying steep hill, the falling began anew. It got worse when, halfway down, his rear binding broke. Amiably Stoned's solution didn't inspire much hope: "I guess you're going to have to ride down on one foot, bro." The writer figures he fell maybe a hundred times before he got down the remaining half a hill. He ended up spending the rest of his vacation in bed, groaning in pain.

The writer had not been informed about what clothes and equipment he would need to get before the lesson. No one told him that he'd need special waterproof gloves, for example—not a comfortable lesson to learn. Or that wrist guards might be a good idea. Or a helmet. He swore he'd never try snowboarding again. Thankfully, I got him to give it one more chance. Today, my writer friend snowboards like a pro. Without falling.

I've heard so many variations on that first-lesson horror story from my students, I can't remember them all. But now there's hope. Whether you want to try advanced tricks, challenging backcountry freeriding, or just hope to get to the bottom in one piece, why not try the most safe and effective method? You'll only get better. My no-fall method is designed to help *all* riders become more confident on any terrain, regardless of their previous boarding experience—or lack of. The information in this book will prepare you for every situation you might encounter on the slopes, along with any variation in gradient and pitch. Nothing can be more intimidating than taking that very first step, but that no longer has to be the case.

Just the Facts, Ma'am . . .

The truth is, winter sports are relatively safe: in 2001, there were only 45 fatalities reported from both skiing and snowboarding combined. Compare that to fatality rates from other, more common recreational pursuits:

In 2000, there were 91 deaths associated with scuba diving. That's nearly twice as many as skiing and snowboarding—yet there are only 1.6 million scuba divers compared to 10.7 million skiers and snowboarders. Boating registered 701 fatalities out of 12.8 million boaters, and bicycling had 800 associated deaths out of nearly 40 million participants. In 2001, swimming claimed almost 22 fatalities per million or so swimmers. In 2000, however, snowboarding and skiing *together* averaged only 4.21 fatalities per every million participants. As far as snow sports go, snowboarding is thought to be even safer than skiing in some ways: "In terms of fatal injuries, snowboarding is considered much safer than skiing" stated a National Ski Areas Association study ("Facts About Skiing/Snowboarding Safety," www.nsaa.org).

Experts also agree that snowboarding doesn't deserve its stereotypical image as the ultimate danger to skiers. According to Dr. Jasper Shealy, a Rochester Institute of Technology professor with three decades of investigating snow-sport-associated injuries under his belt, only 2.6 percent of skier-related injuries involve snowboarding. "Snowboarders don't appear to be making the slopes less safe for their skiing peers, either," Dr. Shealy notes ("Facts About Skiing/Snowboarding Safety," www.nsaa.org). Still, injuries that can result from careless snowboarding are real—they may not kill you, but they're indeed serious. Hence the need for a no-fall snowboarding method that *works*.

Wrist fractures are snowboarding's number-one injury. According to a decade-spanning survey conducted by Vail-Summit Orthopaedics and Sports Medicine, wrist injuries make up 21.6 percent of all snowboard-related injuries. The results of a broken wrist can linger for your entire life; even a wrist *sprain* can prove a chronic lifelong injury.

The good news is that keeping your wrist safe is easy: it's all about riding smart. "Wrist guards may be a snowboarders best friend," concludes Vail-Summit Orthopaedics' study. Indeed, the wrist guard option makes for good sense. In a study by the New Hampshire Knee Center, of almost 2,400 beginner snowboarders observed, those who wore "wrist guards did not sustain any wrist, hand, elbow or shoulder injuries"; out of those that forwent wrist guards, there were forty wrist injuries, consisting of twenty-two sprains and eighteen fractures.

But there's something else you can do to prevent wrist injury, too:

you can choose to snowboard without falling, making the threat of wrist injury almost obsolete.

Snowboarding without falling also helps avoid hurting the number-two place to injure oneself in snowboarding: the coccyx, or tailbone. If you butt-slam hard enough, you can break or bruise your tailbone badly enough to be reminded of it forever—a long-ass time, so to speak. Now *that's* pain, no doubt about that. Then there's what killed Sonny Bono while skiing—fatally crashing into a tree. Or a boulder. Or hard ice. "Doing a Sonny Bono" is, in fact, the ultimate pain reliever. It's pretty hard to feel pain when you're . . . dead. Hence the need for a no-fall snowboarding system that *really works*.

My Story: Snowboarding and Me

I wish I could tell you that my motivation to develop a method of snowboarding free of tumbles and pain initially began with a desire to end all injury, save people, and turn the snow-covered peaks into oases of safety. It wasn't. Like the Financier Icon I mentioned earlier, I was mostly concerned with making money. My method of fall-free snowboarding actually grew out of my desire to obtain as much cash as possible while leading the life of an itinerant snowboard bum.

In truth, I was anything *but* a bum. While living and learning in the life of a snowboarder, I've also worked as an accountant and personal trainer; as well, I've studied martial arts and played Division 2-level college sports. Most significant of all, I have a college degree in business, which has made me very careful about my finances. And on the money tip, there's something that most people who take snowboard or ski lessons don't know: if an instructor gets a student to come back for a repeat lesson, that instructor receives nearly *twice the pay* for all ensuing lessons with that client. I noticed that the students that fell the least were the most likely to sign up for repeat lessons, so I started to tailor my teaching style to cut down on tumbles.

During lessons, I became the human equivalent of training wheels: I'd ride with my back foot out of the binding while holding the student's back hand. Doing this prevented my students from falling, helping them maintain a proper riding position until they developed their skills and confidence enough to be comfortable enough riding on their own.

That didn't prove quite enough, though. A student might feel ready to ride unassisted, but just one butt-slam might cause all that built-up confidence to evaporate into the thin mountain air. So I began to study how snowboarding itself was being taught. Were the boarding techniques imparted to students the right ones? I know every one of those techniques, learning about them from both horror stories via my disgruntled students, and in my own experience learning to ride.

I've been snowboarding for sixteen years, which is about as long as the snowboarding culture as we know it has been percolating around the mainstream. Before I began my lifelong affair with snowboarding, however, I was an obsessive skier. If I could ski hardcore all day, every day, I was *stoked*. That's all I wanted to do.

To pursue that end, I moved to Big Sky, Montana, home to some of the steepest, most thrilling ski terrain in the continental United States. I got a job as a night auditor for a local Big Sky hotel, spending all my free time up on the mountain. I'm always up early to be the first to catch the untracked snow—and you never know who you'll encounter on that first lift ride of the day.

Early one such morning, my friend Dan (no relation) and I were on the chairlift when we saw a strange sight: three guys making their way down the mountain with both feet strapped to a plank. We had never seen anything like what they were doing. As we considered ourselves the most hardcore, aggressive, risk-taking skiers in the world, snowboarding looked like a challenge we couldn't pass up.

The next day, I made the deal of my life with the local equipment-rental dude: if I bought one of his seven rental boards, he'd toss in a free lesson. Well, that was one bargain I just couldn't pass up: a free (well, free-*ish*) snowboard lesson! With our new boards and "teacher" in tow, Dan and I jumped onto the chairlift, taking it all the way to the top of the peak. We managed to make it off the lift in one piece, and then the fun began.

There hadn't been any snow for a few days, so the terrain was pretty used up. Furthermore, the run we chose was an intermediate "blue" run, ungroomed and full of big mogul bumps to boot. Being young and dumb, we set off down the run—at speed, naturally, even though we'd never been on a snowboard before in our lives.

Within 100 yards, Dan and I collided. It was an historic moment—my first ever snowboard wipeout! Dan spit a few times to check for any blood from internal injuries; I believe I loosened all my fillings. In a way, I can still feel the impact today.

Actually, I think the only reason I kept going after that pain was the feeling of immortality and adrenaline that's a defining characteristic of reckless youth. After that collision, my brain was kinda fuzzy; all I could make out was the erstwhile shopowner-cum-snowboard instructor yelling "Turn! Turn! Turn!" like he was in the Byrds. That bit, in fact, was pretty much the full extent of his teaching. At the end of the day, my body *hurt*. I was all beat up and bruised.

Of course, I couldn't wait to do it again.

One time for me, however, ended up being a nightmare I still can't shake. Okay, I'll admit it—I kinda lied a few paragraphs ago when I said I developed my no-fall snowboarding technique strictly out of a desire for, to paraphrase ABBA, "money, money, money." I fully committed myself to no-fall snowboarding after experiencing the most traumatic event in my snowboarding life, the moment that ultimately pushed me to write this book. Early on in my earliest snowboarding days (*daze?*) I was responsible, directly or indirectly, for causing someone very close to me to have an accident that would stay with him for his entire life.

When I started boarding, it was a sport young enough so that, once you were able to get down a mountain without killing yourself, you were an "expert." Imagine the Wright brothers trying to do a loop-de-loop their first time up in the air—that was my m.o. in the old-school snowboarding days. Being an early-twentysomething know-it-all jagoff with zero physical fear further elevated my so-called "expert" status in my own mind. Before long I was teaching all my friends how to do this new, exciting sport.

One day early on, I was teaching my friend Tim. Thanks to my inexperience, he crashed and severely chipped his tailbone during our lesson—an injury that still troubles him (and me) a decade and a half later. It haunts me that I was responsible, however indirectly, for causing a permanent injury in a friend, or anyone for that matter.

In a way, I think my guilt over that incident planted a seed in my mind: I became increasingly devoted to finding a better, safer way to ride the mountain. If I was going to teach people how to snowboard, they weren't going to hurt themselves because of poor instruction. I couldn't have that on my conscience. It sounds kind of corny, but it's true. Of course, not everybody has such a conscience—especially the people most likely to teach you snowboarding, which I discovered as my career as a snowboard instructor progressed.

How Did We Get Here?

There are seemingly as many variations on teaching snowboarding as there are snowboard instructors. One student told me she was taught the "pet the dog, sit on the chair" riding method: in other words, as you snowboard, you mimic the motions of petting a dog and sitting on a chair in order to turn. It's like some misguided riff on *The Karate Kid*'s "wash the car" routine. When I taught in Australia, they favored the "little teapot" approach, as in the song: "I'm a little teapot/Short and stout/Here is my handle/Here is my spout/So tip me over and pour some out." Believe it or not, Australian snowboard instructors teach their students to act out this song and pretend they are little teapots while riding in order to make the so-called "proper" movements for snowboarding. Seriously.

These were the very kind of techniques I myself absorbed first as a beginning boarder and then as a snowboarding instructor. In fact, to this day I must take regular courses in these techniques to remain fully accredited by the American Association of Snowboard Instructors, which means I'm qualified to teach at any resort in the world.

If you want to teach snowboarding, you *must* remain accredited in AASI's methods, even if you don't agree that they're the best way to ride. Just consider a recent ad promoting the American Association of Snowboard Instructors in its own trade magazine, *The Pro Rider*. Across the top of the page a headline proclaimed in bolded, full-cap *gravitas*, **"YOUR STUDENTS WILL FALL."**

In other words, even the people *officially* certified to teach you to snowboard safely take falling as a given. Like Ms. "Snowboarding is *Pain!*," they see falling as almost a rite of passage, and believe that only those who can endure the hurt are tough enough to join the cool-kids snowboarding club. Think about it: is *that* who you want to learn snowboarding from?

I found embedded in the snowboard-teaching culture a number of strange contradictions that can make learning to ride potentially hazardous to your health. In order to get the best instructor jobs, it's advantageous to be accredited by teachers who indoctrinate you in methods I outright reject; you can't even take their exams if you don't work for an affiliated ski school. The problem is, those in charge of this accreditation aren't typically snowboarders but . . . *skiers*.

That skiers dominate snowboard instruction is all about supply and demand—more and more, people are opting to learn to snowboard over taking beginning ski lessons, so ski instructors switch-hit just to maintain the lifestyle to which they've become accustomed. I know this to be true because I helped Mr. Super Bowl Rings' instructor get her accreditation. At that point, the demand for snowboarding instructors was so great, they had to utilize idle ski instructors to take on the overflow of lessons.

I was her tutor: she, a ski instructor, had not yet finished her accreditation to teach snowboarding, yet she had somehow been assigned a plum celebrity client like Mr. Super Bowl Rings. She had to cram and pass the snowboarding test, in fact, to keep the celebrity appointment; I helped her cram, mostly because she was cute. Like, say, the requirement to parallel park to pass a driving exam, in this instance each new snowboarding instructor had to know how to snowboard backwards.

Well, just two weeks before her lesson with Mr. Super Bowl Rings, his instructor didn't know how to ride backwards, and the test loomed. I spent a February afternoon teaching her how to ride backwards. She *was* cute. Anyway, the point of this whole ramble is that Mr. Super Bowl Rings was, in fact, Ms. Test Crammer's *first* snowboarding student. *Ever.* That's how he lost his snowboarding virginity: a most famous student gets stuck with the least experienced member of its snowboard-teaching team—someone who's really more skier than snowboarder. Unfortunately, that's still all too typical.

There are three levels of certification offered by the American Association of Snowboard Instructors; Level 3 instructors hold the most training and experience (I'm Level 3). Do you know who teaches beginning snowboarding on most mountains? Level 1 instructors—in other words, the most inexperienced snowboarders typically teach the most inexperienced students to ride. In fact, the snowboard instructor you're learning from may not be accredited at all.

I don't know about you, but when I'm learning something for the first time, I want to be sure I'm learning from the most seasoned expert available. Studies show first-time snowboarder students are at increased risk for injury (Paul J. Abbot, *The American Journal of Sports Medicine*, January 1, 2004): the Medical College of Wisconsin confirms that "beginning snowboarders are the most frequently injured even though they attempt less dangerous maneuvers than advanced snowboarders. Nearly 25 percent of injuries occur during a snowboarder's first experience and almost one-half occur during the first season of snowboarding" (www.healthlink .mcw.edu). Almost anyone who's tried snowboarding has a story about injuring themselves while learning, even as snowboarding remains the most vital winter sport.

Snowboarding's success may also prove to be its downfall. Snowboarding is a very young sport, and in the snow-sports establishment, skiers are deeply entrenched. So, when snowboarding began to take off, it was the skiers who had the infrastructure and power to really capitalize on its success, and who took over its teaching.

Ironically, snowboarding has proven a bigger influence on skiing than vice versa: today's parabolic skis, whose enhanced sidecut makes turning so easy compared to their predecessors, can trace their technical improvements to the incorporation of snowboarding innovations. And today's freestyle-ski hotdoggers more than anything evoke the gravity-defiant moves of freestyle boarders getting big air.

Skiing's monopoly over snow-sport culture has made a deep impact on snowboard instruction, though. The professional associations of skiing instructors took over the accreditation of snowboarding instructors. As a result, the teaching method institutionalized at resorts all over the world is based more on the idea that snowboarding is like skiing on one ski than on the actual experience of snowboarding. This became all too clear to me in my experience as a staff instructor at various big resorts throughout America (and at Mount Buller, Australia, too). But skiers aren't the only people responsible for messing up snowboarding—they often get help from snowboarders themselves.

Let us return to the story of Mr. Financial Icon. Remember him, the

Wall Street bigshot who ended his first snowboard lesson carted off the mountain by paramedics? Well, I knew his instructor, too; he's a buddy of mine. From now on, we shall refer to him as "Wolfgang."

Wolfgang is no skier; he's one of the most hardcore snowboarders I know. Wolfgang snowboards whenever he can, always doing something extreme on a board—typically *too* extreme. Wolfgang endorses only one method of snowboarding: "bombing." That is, he rides the board flat and straight down the fall line as fast as possible, ending in a big stop. Skilled riders can "bomb" reasonably safely, and it sure is fun. As a general approach, however, bombing is probably not the best choice for a beginner, especially when he's a rich and famous septuagenarian. I know my technique could've helped Mr. Super Bowl Rings and Mr. Financial Icon, and even more "expert" riders, too.

Before my very first job I was told by my supervising instructor to expect only *12 percent* of first-time snowboarders to return for further lessons. The remaining 88 percent, he told me, were too scared to come back. That didn't make economic sense to my business-major mind. Why not try to get as many people as possible to come back for a second lesson—or third, or fourth, even? An article on winter-sport injuries states "the success of any sport relies on its ability to attract and retain new participants. . . . The risk of injury as a result of an alpine snow sport is much lower than commonly perceived, with one injury occurring approximately every 300 days of participation. However, if that injury occurs early on in a person's experience, the individual may be understandably reluctant to ever contemplate a return to the sport concerned" (*The American Journal of Sports Medicine*, Paul J. Abbott, January 1, 2004). This analysis makes the problem clear: there's a limit to how many people are willing to fall while learning to snowboard, and if the falling doesn't stop, the sport will suffer. I just can't accept the industry willfully shrinking itself.

So my road-testing of no-fall snowboarding began in earnest. I began incorporating my no-fall snowboard methods into my lessons, thinking they might draw more, and different, students to ride. My experiment met with *huge* success. Once my students stopped falling, they continually requested me as their instructor, and they referred their friends to me as well.

The real reason I want you to adopt no-fall snowboarding is simply this: I love snowboarding. Snowboarding does have a way of turning its practitioners into evangelists for the sport. That's because, once you try it, you find snowboarding lives up to its advance hype. It's exciting, it's about speed and the wind in your face as you spirit skillfully down steep grades. But in many ways, snowboarding also has the benefits of, say, yoga. It's meditative, calming. It makes you more aware of your environment, as well as your body. It brings out the physical grace that's within all of us: with time and dedication, you'll discover your body can do things that you never thought were possible.

The Benefits: Mind, Body, and Soul

Snowboarding is incredible exercise. The day I wrote these words, I looked into the mirror and saw a forty-one-year-old; however, I'm in better shape than I was when I was sixteen. I'm not lying when I say snowboarding keeps me young, and it'll keep you young, too.

For one, doing any kind of exercise in a high-altitude mountain setting provides an incredible extra workout for your cardiovascular system, without you having to do anything extra in your routine. That's because high-altitude atmospheric environments carry the fitness benefit of thinner air. When you are in thinner air, your heart works harder to get the same amount of oxygen circulating in your blood that it would in lower altitudes—and in so doing it develops more healthy muscle.

When you add exercise to being in a high altitude, the heart gets even stronger. Remember how Superman got superpowers because the gravity on his home planet Krypton was so strong, that when he got to Earth's weaker gravity field, he could fly? Well, giving your heart a high-altitude workout makes it work better especially when you return to lower altitudes. Alternatively, exercising your cardiovascular system in low altitudes best prepares the heart to work at higher performance in elevated altitudes. Having become stronger up high, in lower altitudes your heart muscle can now work more efficiently. The heart now can push much more oxygen through the bloodstream to where it's needed much more easily. Just by snowboarding, and doing nothing else, your heart is getting a supreme workout.

Such training also vastly contributes to long-term cardiovascular health. These health-fitness benefits are why some gyms in New York City and Los Angeles now feature special exercise/training areas scientifically engineered to simulate high-altitude atmospheric conditions. Other gyms worldwide are following their high-altitude lead as well. And did you know the body burns more calories in colder weather, too?

All this is further proof that snowboarding is just good for heart and health in many ways. And as your skills improve, snowboarding's aerobic benefits expand additionally as well.

Depending on one's weight and how hard one chooses to ride, one can burn anywhere from 400 to 800 calories per hour snowboarding (those of us that regularly dig ourselves out of being stuck in a few feet of powder snow would unscientifically put that number at closer to 1,000 calories). Compare that to gym aerobics (roughly 600 calories per hour on the high end), yoga (around 340 calories burned per hour), weight lifting/gym strength training (517 calories per hour), golf (474 calories per hour, but only if you carry your bags), and rollerblading (430 calories per hour).

Incredibly, surfing, that most intense and extreme sport, burns a mere 258 calories an hour, a surprisingly small amount compared to snowboarding's burn rate (sport-specific calorie-burning conversion tables courtesy www.self.com). "With snowboarding, you are going to access some of that fat storage and burn it up," Eddie Graham explains. "There's caloric expenditure on the hill: your skin is going to get closer to muscle, and you'll have more of a lean look."

Yup, snowboarding is just good for overall body health, period. Because snowboarding is a balance sport, your abdominal muscles are going to get a real workout—the kind Hollywood stars take pilates classes for. You'll find it's a lot easier maintaining that coveted six-pack if you put snowboarding into your life. Every time you stand up after sitting on a snowboard, your abs get solidly crunched. And as you balance on a snowboard, you're using your back and stomach muscles to keep stable, stretching and strengthening them in the process.

But that's not all: your knees will thank you, too. Snowboarding correctly makes knee injury quite unlikely, so you can avoid the knee wear-and-tear impact you might receive running or playing tennis, for example. Your butt, arms, and legs (especially the hamstrings and "quad" muscles) will thank you too. And for what? Increased tone, performance, and flexibility.

Balance sports also tend to advance agility and response. My students talk frequently about how their reflexes seem quicker after snowboarding regularly, how they notice their capacity for exercise endurance expands by leaps and bounds.

With these benefits, if you're anywhere near a mountain, why would you ever need a gym? A gym is great for fitness when living in the city, and for getting ready to snowboard. But snowboarding is where I found my peak physical performance. After a day of snowboarding, my body is so warmed up, I feel like I'm back in the shape I was while wrestling back in college, only now I don't have to wear tights at all (unless I *really, really* want to, of course).

Snowboarding for me is ultimately about faith—faith that what I'm doing is good for me and the world. I hope learning what I've learned will help you believe, too. With faith, your dedication will result in tangible results. Your body will look better. You'll feel better.

I know all this might be hard to take at first. When I began studying martial arts, the instructors would talk about the mystical oneness of the soul, how the balance you'll learn will help you balance your life, and so on. I thought it sounded like propaganda—follow all this blindly, and your life will be perfect. But despite my initial skepticism, I found that devoting myself to martial arts made me more balanced in both body and soul. Further on down the line, I discovered that snowboarding can have the same effect.

The No-Fall
Snowboarding Promise

There are countless ways to get down a hill, but ultimately I believe mine is the best way. You see, my aspiration is to be the *Consumer Reports* of snowboarding. I grew up on *Consumer Reports* magazine. Throughout childhood, I was surrounded by *Consumer Reports*–approved washing machines, kitchen appliances, even bicycles. My dad would only make purchases after checking the reviews by its incorruptible editorial staff. Getting only the most reliable, road-tested items was Dad's effort to perfect our existence in the world. In that spirit, I can't imagine teaching snowboarding without offering the best no-fall alternative possible.

As I developed my methods, I discovered that most snowboarding manuals and books tried to be all things to all people, and ultimately failed to serve anyone very well. My no-fall technique, on the other hand, offers a simple, elegant template that's easy to master with minimal instruction—just the necessary tools.

My promise: follow my seven easy steps to snowboarding correctly, and you *will* become a snowboarder. One who doesn't fall. That's what I think people long for in that initial snowboard lesson, and that's what I give you here.

To my mind, this book does something no other snowboarding tome I know of has attempted successfully: it shows you the technique in a way that you can practice at home. That's right—you'll start learning *before* you've bought the plane tickets, before you've strapped in and taken that obligatory, terrifying virgin chairlift ride. This way, the movements and stances that make up no-fall snowboarding become instinctual before you ever even hit snow. As a result, you'll shorten your learning curve on the mountain, ride more safely, and get the most out of your time on the slopes.

In reality, though, this book isn't just an instructional manual. It's also my love letter to snowboarding—*real* snowboarding. I'm pretty sure you'll fall in love, too. But enough talk. The sooner we get through these lessons, the sooner we can get on the mountain. That's why we're here, right?

Step 2—Get in Shape

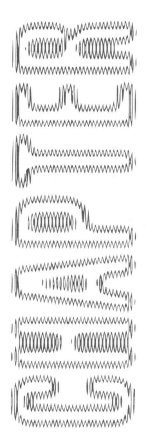

ike many sports, snowboarding is all about the physical preparation you do *before* you hit the mountain. After you commit to the idea that you're becoming a snowboarder, well, getting in shape to ride is job one. A bummer that I've come to expect all too regularly during beginner snowboard lessons rears its ugly head when I ask what physical exercise the student has done to prepare; the answer, far too often, is "none." You, dear reader, are different. You will be ready because this chapter will take you there.

Snowboarding will challenge your body in new ways, so preparation is essential: yes, it's *possible* to get down a mountain on snowboard without getting your body ready, but just because it's possible doesn't make it a good idea. The more stamina and strength the snowboarder has, the quicker the body can react—and the easier it is to learn to snowboard without falling.

Above all, it's best to have an ongoing stretch-workout regimen that gives your body the proper strength and flexibility for optimum riding. I have designed such a regimen that I call my "BYGS"—i.e. "*before* you go snowboarding"—workout: it familiarizes the body with the movements you'll learn later in the book. My stretch-workout routine is succinct, designed to take just *twenty minutes*: in that short time every day, however, you will create all the muscle memory you need on the mountain. Do the BYGS workout now, and you'll easily access all its benefits on the slopes later.

When you actually begin to learn my technique, you'll find having done BYGS has already taught you how to move in the appropriate fashion. And your body will be in the ideal shape for snowboarding. That means it will be in pretty close to ideal shape, *period.* Not a bad fringe benefit!

That's right—rigorously following my physical-training agenda will make your body happier. Snappier, indeed. But if you continue on with snowboarding, you can expect to be hot-rodded into the best physical shape of your life. "There will be a visible difference—snowboarding provides an aesthetic improvement," explains Eddie Graham, an American Council on Exercise certified personal trainer for the acclaimed Equinox gym company and a veteran of training for (and running in) seven New York City Marathons. "The butt and legs just look better after snowboarding. When you're in that crouched position with your knees bent, you get an isometric benefit on your glutes and legs."

Wrestling the Mountain

All the physical activity I've done in my life—from playing football to getting certified as a personal trainer—has proven useful in my development of the no-fall snowboarding program. Aside from martial arts, I've learned the most from wrestling.

I went to college on a wrestling scholarship, where I learned how wrestling can be both primal and noble. Indeed, wrestling has been around since ancient Greece's earliest Olympic games, and some of civilization's greatest thinkers were wrestlers. Plato was a youth wrestling champion; Pythagoras, the father of mathematics as we know it, had an earlier sideline as a frequently victorious Olympic wrestler.

Wrestling is the sport whose lessons I keep returning to as I progress in my snowboarding. Socrates once said "I swear it upon Zeus an outstanding runner cannot be the equal of an average wrestler," and it's true: wrestling first taught me the significance of utmost physical preparedness in sport. "Wrestling is ballet with violence," explained wrestler-turned-politician Jesse "The Body" Ventura in a philosophical moment. But my favorite quote on wrestling comes from that great emperor of ancient Rome, Marcus Aurelius: "The art of living is more like wrestling than dancing, insofar as it stands ready against the accidental and the unforeseen, and is not apt to fall."

Aurelius' take on wrestling is much like my version of snowboarding—it prepares you most readily against the accidental and unforeseen, and is *specifically designed* so you're not apt to fall, either. But I find other parallels between snowboarding and wrestling, too.

At their core, both sports are ultimately more about personal excellence than anything else. Only the individual athlete knows if he has expressed his best performance, and that's all that matters.

No doubt the great thinkers admired wrestling's transformative discipline—the more you do, the better you become—something that wrestling also shares with no-fall snowboarding. In college wrestling, we were always maintaining our weight. To that end, wrestling practice lasted five hours a day, seven days a week, no standing still. It was stretching, drills, and jumping rope, which aids in agility and cardiorespiratory response. Mainly we just wanted to keep our muscles warm all the time. My college wrestling coach said, "You're not going to lose because you're in worse shape than your opponent—you're going to win because you're in *better* shape."

In snowboarding, you're wrestling the mountain, so it's best to be in *better* shape. When I was first learning to snowboard, I wasn't fazed about that falling stuff; after all, I'd been thrown to the mat a few hundred times. I was regularly "souffléed" as such by the toughest wrestlers on the team, or tossed head-first onto the gridiron by a 260-pound linebacker, so my fear of falling disappeared long before I ever strapped on a board; it was literally beaten out of me. In developing my technique, I experimented with every possible sequence of movements until I found a combination that ensured I didn't fall at all. I endured a number of spills along the way—so you don't have to.

BYGS: Why It Works

But whatever sport I was doing, I was always physically prepared. That's how I want you to think of snowboarding, too: the more you can prepare your body beforehand the faster you'll learn, you'll snowboard better *and* get the most out of your time on the hill. But don't worry, you're not going to have to work out for five hours a day like I did as a wrestler. The point is to get your body ready to *snowboard* five hours a day. The workout regimen I've designed will get you into ideal shape, and quickly. "Danny's workout is the total package—a simple, yet challenging, sport-specific program," says personal trainer/marathon man Eddie Graham. "It's just sensible, straightforward, and effective—nothing tricky, no smoke and mirrors."

My ideal BYGS regimen can take as little as twenty minutes—at most just a mere *half-hour* a day, depending on how hardcore you want to be with it. BYGS is designed for maximum user-friendliness, so that you can do any part of it anywhere you wish.

Take that time: to wrestle the mountain to your best advantage on a snowboard, you absolutely want to be in the best shape possible, both mentally and physically. The mountain wants to let you win, but you have to help it do so by playing the game by the mountain's rules. To that end, the BYGS exercises cover all the fitness bases: doing them regularly will get you into optimum snowboarding shape. "It's a *balanced* approach, which I go with myself," Eddie Graham explains. "It works the legs, quads, hamstrings, and calves, along with the lower back, abdominals, chest and shoulders. This kind of balanced workout—strengthening, stretching, fuel—ties it all together."

What Bruce Lee Taught Me About Snowboarding

It didn't surprise me to hear Eddie Graham refer to "balance" as the most important thing in a snowboarding workout. I myself learned the concept of balanced fitness—balanced *everything*—from martial arts.

One person who understood sports fitness in a complete way was my hero, martial-arts legend Bruce Lee. Lee explored and practiced all types of martial arts with an open mind, then took the best bits from all of them. Following his example, I've adapted into my snowboarding technique the best, most applicable lessons learned not just from my years of snowboarding and skiing, but from other physical pursuits as well, notably studying martial arts.

For example, thanks to my martial-arts background, I've incorporated into my snowboarding training a way to maintain 360 degree visual awareness while you ride. Ever seen a Bruce Lee movie? He seems always to anticipate an opponent coming from behind. When I studied *tang soo do*—a Korean martial arts practice that means "way of the Chinese hand"—I finally understood how he did it.

Tang soo do is distinguished by extreme discipline, focus, and emphasis on aggressive attacking and preventive self-defense. *Tang soo do* put everything into crisp focus: I learned that Bruce wasn't just anticipating opponents from behind, he was *seeing* them. As he fought, Lee would look around in every possible direction, gaining a full view of the battlefield, yet doing it so quickly it was imperceptible. That's because Bruce's body was limber and fast enough to go there when necessary. When you train to ride the right way, you'll discover there is no such thing as a snowboarding "blind spot." Your neck can be almost as limber as Bruce Lee's, too. You'll be surprised how aware of your environment you can be while snowboarding in the no-fall style, and how easily that awareness is attained.

My study of *tang soo do* truly pushed me toward not just balanced fitness, but also the path to no-fall snowboarding itself. My martial-arts adventure began during the five glorious years I lived on the Hawaiian island of Maui. I had just graduated college and was working as an accountant in a Maui Ford dealership when I found myself missing the camaraderie, the regimented practice, and most of all the *discipline* of wrestling at an elite level. At the same time, I craved a physical endeavor that offered something more. That's when I discovered martial arts.

I started studying with Master Ron Holland, a *tang soo do* master of *haole* descent (*haole* is a not-so-nice Hawaiian word for "white person"). Master Holland, as his students called him, had grown up on a Native American reservation, but ended up devoting much of his life to studying the martial arts of Asia. Unconfirmed rumors have it that the Kennedy administration commissioned him during the Vietnam War to train marines in hand-to-hand combat.

Not surprisingly, Master Holland was a bit of a Zen hard-ass. And I mean that in the best way. "While you are studying at our Do Jang, you will be challenged, excited, exhausted, sometimes discouraged, frequently triumphant," Master Holland wrote in the manual that accompanied his teachings. "In fact, every feeling you have in the course of your daily life outside the walls of this studio, you will experience during your training. By working through these feelings and emotions during your training, you will learn things that will help you in the other parts of your life."

Heady stuff, but that's exactly what I wanted to fill my head with. I emptied my cup and took in Master Holland's rigor-based instruction. He was about doing. And doing. And *doing again*. Immediately I began to notice martial arts' transformative discipline. As I practiced more, my skills, my reflexes, my body improved and kept improving. The one thing that most influenced my snowboarding instruction from martial arts, however, was its philosophy of balance.

Learning the Art of Balance

In *tang soo do*, every move starts from a rock-solid "ready stance"—the position that you're in where you'll be able to move readily in any direction comfortably, quickly, and stably. If you find yourself on unstable ground during a fight, you can always return to the ready stance for your next move. And in training your body to be balanced and alert at all times, such balance gradually becomes second nature. Soon, everything in life appears to take on greater balance.

In the *doing*, I found that such emphasis on balance proved to be absolutely correct. But when I moved to Colorado to snowboard after my intense martial-arts study in Hawaii, something felt . . . *off.* I no longer felt as balanced on a snowboard as I did, say, in the "ready stance" at the core of *tang soo do.* If I was going to be on a snowboard, I needed to feel as balanced and as in control of my actions and reactions as I did studying martial arts.

After learning *tang soo do*, it didn't make sense to me that you would snowboard any way but balanced from around your center. The notion accepted among my snowboard-instructor peers is that letting gravity drag your center around every which way is the right way to ride. Following my martial-arts study, that concept seemed suddenly, well, *unbalanced*. I was determined to find a teachable method of snowboarding where balance is king, and falling is not an issue. Furthermore, I wanted my students' actual riding to be better in every way—both on the mountain and off it.

"Another important benefit is a sense of inner peace, derived from our art because we practice it away from the hectic environment of our daily routines," wrote Master Holland on what is perhaps the ultimate gain of both snowboarding and martial arts. I have devoted my life to snowboarding for the same reason many turn to religion or meditation: inner peace.

Snowboarding just seemed like the most efficient way to achieve as unhectic and contemplative a daily routine as possible. Snowboarding has become my favorite sport, in fact, because it takes me out of the race. Strapped to a snowboard, the rider alone becomes the coach, the team, and the finish line all in one. "Winning," in the traditional sense, becomes irrelevant; just balancing on that plank is the greatest success. As Bruce Lee said himself, "Unless you realize what life is about, right now some game is happening . . . Most people can be blinded by it."

Learning the Art of Breathing

In all martial arts, the first thing one does is learn to breathe. I figured I already knew how to breathe, but I was wrong. As in yoga, martial-arts practice commences by teaching the student to regiment and strengthen breathing. You begin by concentrating solely on breathing, taking in oxygen in measured bursts through your nose, filling your lungs.

Techniques for exhaling differ across disciplines. Martial-arts tradition teaches inhaling through the nose but exhaling fully through the mouth, as the oral exhale adds an extra burst of power to the corresponding movement. In yoga, many teachers suggest students attempt to control the inhale and exhale solely through the nostrils. Both yoga and martial arts use conscious, strategic breathing for the same end purpose, however: to control and distribute the energy created by the breath. Try experimenting with both approaches to see their different results.

This strategic breathing process blocks out all unnecessary stimuli in your environment. When I'm in line at the grocery store with five people in front of me—all of whom have ignored the "ten items or less" sign I practive my breathing and balance. As I wait to pay, I instinctively, almost subconsciously rehearse the breathing sequence that gets me back into alignment. Once you can control and regulate your breathing, it's suddenly easier to control and regulate your other body responses as well. You can imagine how important that ability is making quick decisions as you rocket down the hill on a snowboard.

"Rehearsing" the Body for Ultimate Snowboarding

In the teaching of acting, some methods insist that you know all your lines before you even start rehearsing, so you can focus strictly on the most important task at hand. Famed playwright/screenwriter/director David Mamet and his Atlantic Theater Company incorporate this super-prepared approach to acting. This is something they share with the classical English acting tradition that produced the bad-ass likes of Laurence Olivier. This approach makes rehearsal immediately creative—what you're doing is the real work, not just worrying about whether you remember your line or not. You're *doing* right away.

Similarly, it's time to begin teaching your muscles their "lines." This is the process that encodes your muscle memory with the training and stretch movements that will prove most useful on the mountain.

Even if you snowboard for just one week a year, but you regularly do all the training I've laid out here, then you're going to be ready to go snowboarding any time—which means you're going to be in perfect shape *all the time*. To paraphrase modernist architect Mies van der Rohe, your form will finally follow any function your mind sets it to.

This is not an impossible process. On bookstore shelves and in Amazon.com searches, one constantly encounters titles like "The Ultimate Fifteen-Second Super-Ab Workout." Well, you don't necessarily need the ultimate *anything* to get into shape. If all you can spare is five minutes at first to work out, that already is a whole lot. More would be better, but just going for it *at all* is what's most crucial.

You'll also find that your body's ability—and desire—to do more will increase gradually, at your own pace. After three weeks of doing my BYGS stretch-workout regimen, you'll discover that you are stronger. That your stature is different. Your body will hold itself differently just from the attention you've been giving it. Chances are you'll begin to feel more, yes, *balanced.*

All you need to do my BYGS exercises is the ground underneath your feet, and maybe a wall. Wherever that ground may be found, you can do this training—in the comfort of your own home, or any other place of your choosing. Even some places that may not exactly be of your choosing are okay: as Master Holland used to say, physical preparation "can be done anywhere, even in a jail cell." Later in the book, at a point when you hopefully will be ready to snowboard, you'll see I've also adapted my exercises and stretches in an "On The Mountain" (OTM) workout specifically designed for when you actually get to the mountain. In other words, I've designed my OTM sequence to be performed entirely outdoors, on the hill, in the riding environment. I figure if you've gone to the effort to get to the mountain, you should interact as much as possible with that magical natural environment. Why hang out in your living room and do your routine at home when you can be on the mountain? The more time you spend on the hill, the more comfortable you'll be on snow.

To that user-friendly, go-anywhere end, I've designed my physical-training sequences to serve two functions. First, they are the ultimate preparation for no-fall snowboarding in advance of going to the mountain. The more you do them before you actually get on the snow, the more prepared your body will be to absorb the instruction and perform my method. Second, my BYGS and OTM regimens can be used as ongoing fitness conditioning to keep you in ideal snowboarding shape. They're easily expandable and adaptable to your own comfort zone.

Enough with the pep talk. Let's get right to the exercises that will get you ready for snowboarding. My BYGS workout here mimics exactly the physical preparation that I do every day, both for my own fitness and to get my students in the right physical shape for instruction.

It's based on training your muscles for balance. If you balance via your muscles, your riding is going to be that much more stable and your body will be able to react quicker. Each muscle, you see, helps the other muscles. In order to move smoothly, your muscles need to be relaxed so the energy flows through your body.

Just as in martial arts, in both no-fall snowboarding and my workout you want to make each move effective. You want to move your body in a proper series of movements that follow how your muscles create balance.

See, the energy in your body moves from one muscle to the next, and on to the next after that. It's like a chain reaction: if one of your muscles is tight, the flow is interrupted—the energy stops at that one little tight muscle. "You're only as strong as your weakest link," Eddie Graham confirms. "Balance is functional training. It makes complete sense. You want symmetry: you don't want your calves out of symmetry with your anterior deltoids. You want everything matched and working together. This enables the person who wants to get out there snowboarding to actually be able to accomplish it."

Now I want you to find out for yourself the many benefits of my BYGS stretch-workout sequence. On the hill, you're going to be stretching continuously as you snowboard. Every time you stop, you'll find you almost subconsciously need to stretch a little bit somewhere. Your body will tell you what muscles need attention. Believe me, if you do sit-ups and push-ups everyday, take walks and stretch regularly, then you will be better positioned for life, not to mention a mere snowboard lesson. *Please*, find out for yourself. It's easy.

So, onward, my friend. As I said before, it's what I do every day *and* what I have my students do prior to their first snowboarding lessons.

A Note About Safety When Starting a New Workout Program

My snowboarding workout has been designed so that even a total novice at physical exercise can do it. As trainer/athlete Eddie Graham noted earlier, almost *anyone* should be able to attempt my snowboard workout, within the reasonable limits of size, age, weight, and health.

However, if you think you need to get a clearance from a physician before attempting any exercise program *for any reason*, please do so. If you have severe neck or knee problems, or feel discomfort in any portion of these stretches or flexes, discontinue the exercise immediately.

Everyone, however, should always be careful to limber up slowly. Start at a level *you* feel good at; only hold a move that feels good to *you*. There's no reason anyone should feel pain from a warm-up. That said, if you generally find my BYGS workout sequence painful, then you're probably not in the right shape to go snowboarding, for whatever reason.

If you are unable to complete the majority of this sequence, check in with your doctor. Everyone's health and lifestyle is different.

The "Ultimate" BYGS Workout (Actually, It's Pretty Easy . . .)

This is a sequence that is designed for ease of use. It can be performed as a single, flowing, uninterrupted groove, like a yoga lesson that seamlessly links beginning, middle, and end.

Speaking of yoga, consider getting a yoga mat of your own to do your snowboard exercises on. A yoga mat can be thrown down anywhere, protecting you from dirty floors while you exercise. At the same time, a yoga mat can transform any space, even that jail cell, into a gym. Rolling out that mat triggers a response that it's time for your body to get down to business and work out. "Using a yoga mat can transform a whole area," Eddie Graham says. "It changes it into *your* workout area."

Remember, take it at *your* speed. If you need to, at first you can approach building my workout sequence modularly. Begin with just one exercise or stretch that you think you can manage; then start gradually pushing your limits. Add more to your workout as your body becomes attuned to working out. Start with walking, then add additional elements when you feel comfortable moving to the next stage.

I'd rather you do some kind of regular workout than none at all; if all you can muster is a five-minute walk and a back stretch, your life will improve noticeably. But do try to complete the whole darn thing, please. Often when you're riding on the hill, you'll find you almost subconsciously need to stretch continuously: my physical training will tell you what you need to do.

Best of all, snowboard training is *democratic*, baby. Sure, going to the gym and getting a full, professional workout regularly is great. Pilates and yoga especially are excellent boarding body prep. Aerobics classes would surely be a great addition to what I recommend you do here.

With my simple BYGS plan, anybody can tackle the basics of getting into snowboarding shape—and be better for it, whatever your athletic interest. "With a strong and flexible core, you can throw harder, hit harder in swing sports like tennis and golf, and perform better in such solos sports as climbing, kayaking, skiing, and snowboarding," writes Curtis

Pesmen in a May 2004 *Esquire* fitness column. "The anchor of your appendages enables each and all of them to coil, fire, and follow through more completely. . . . You literally can no longer afford to perform half-assed. Or misaligned."

Strategic Breathing

Doing this helps the whole enchilada—but strategic breathing can *really* help muscles used in a particular stretch or workout.

How Long Should I Do This?

It's up to you, but I recommend breathing all the time. Hey, that's what I do.

Before we start exercising, however, we need to talk about breathing; in fact, it's a good idea to practice your breathing even while you walk. That's right—*practice* your breathing. Above all, you want to train your body to *control* and *direct* your breath. Unless you've studied yoga or martial arts, you probably never thought about breathing as something one practices, let alone controls. Breathing seems like, well, the most natural, instinctual thing in the world—the one thing you don't have to think about. It's going to happen anyway, right?

Breathing, however, is the secret to many world-class athletes' success. Watch reruns of your favorite Olympics event—Kenyan long-distance runners taking all the gold in 2004, say, with their famous endurance and gliding dexterity—and really focus on how those champion athletes breathe. I'm betting it's regular, even, and one with their stride. That's what we're aspiring to, and it's within our reach.

Breathing is even more important in snow sports: remember, if you're snowboarding, most likely you're doing it at a high altitude. Because there's less oxygen at higher altitudes, learning strategic breathing while you exercise before you snowboard will simulate and enhance the oxygen intake you'll need when you're on the mountain.

A. Begin by taking several slow, deep breaths.
B. Try making your inhale last for about four to six seconds, then hold it for a second more before exhaling. Attempt to regulate your exhale so it takes the same time to let the air out as it did to suck it in.
C. Try to get your breathing into a rhythm that feels good; explore extending and varying the amount of time you're able to inhale and exhale. You might be surprised to find yourself able to maintain long, flowing breaths that can last up to fifteen seconds.

Getting used to strategic breathing is essential: you're going to be taking controlled breaths at least two or three times in each different exercise segment of the BYGS workout. Controlled, healthy, *strategic* breathing is the spine of any good fitness regime, and mine is no different. Getting your breathing down will give you energy you didn't know you had.

The Five-Minute Walk

Doing this helps your legs, obviously. But walking also warms up your body's whole circulation system, getting the oxygen in your blood dancing.

How Long Should I Do This?

Well, it *is* called the "five-minute walk." But the longer you walk, the better. . . .

If you start your day with a five-minute walk, you'll be surprised at how good a start that is. In no time, you'll be feeling better than you did, which jibes with the latest medical research on walking's health benefits.

Start examining your everyday routine: look out for walkable distances that you could attempt on foot instead of, say, driving. Try walking to work instead of taking the subway. Think of this five-minute walk as a journey, one where you empty your cup before everyday life begins. It doesn't matter where you walk, what time of day it is, or who you walk with. Try to maintain your level of exertion through your amble, increasing it gradually each day.

Walking on its own burns three hundred calories per hour. Therefore, walking briskly a few times per week could result in shedding up to *two pounds* of unwanted body bulk in a month's time. Walking also works different muscles than running or biking. Walking burns *fat*, while running and cycling use up carbohydrates.

If you can eventually expand that five-minute meander into an everyday one-hour walk, doctors say you could add another *whole decade* to your lifespan. But sparing anywhere from five to ten minutes for walking is good enough for our purposes here.

That's absolutely good enough, in fact. What's even better about walking is what you can get done in just five minutes. Walking the dog, taking the garbage out, going to the store for some more spinach—as far as I'm concerned, all those can count towards your five-minute walk.

Take that time to achieve something you've been putting off so that you commence your workout by getting something *done*.

Many of the balancing movements we use when we walk are echoed in my no-fall snowboarding technique. Walking is when we are most stable in motion, so it's natural that those movements would translate to no-fall snowboarding. You'll see . . .

Every time one of us straps onto a snowboard, we're taking a meditative journey into the unknown. There's no better time to start your journey than right now with a walk. You never do know where your journeys might take you. Raised by a family of accountants in the small town of Devils Lake, North Dakota, I never thought I'd be gainfully employed as a globe-trotting snowboarder. The possibilities I've discovered are endless. Who knows where this particular journey we're taking together with a warm-up walk on your first-ever day training to snowboard will end up?

Take, for example, a married duo I've been working with for years. Their progress as beginning snowboarders astounded me: just one year after I began teaching them, we were taking helicopter trips together to isolated glaciers in the Alps to ride fresh, untracked snow. That's right— they're well into middle age and doing it more extreme than most. In terms of the mythology of *The Matrix*, they took the blue pill and rode that ride until its natural conclusion, exploring their skills' maximum potential. Now let's see how deep that rabbit hole is for *you*. All right?

Walking Stairs

Doing this helps super-condition the leg muscles, strengthening them, and helps prevent leg injuries—in addition to aerobic benefits. In an intense-condensed way, it provides a good overall workout for riding.

How Long Should I Do This?

Two minutes to start—but the more the better. Just listen to your legs, *brah* . . .

Let's get the next phase of this workout going with a bang—a bang-up jaunt up the stairs. Contain your excitement, now! Oh, I know: to many, stairs are an inconvenience, a hassle, but to snowboarders stairs are a blessing in disguise. A stair session is perfect fitness prep for snowboarding and great as an all-around warmer-upper, too. "The stairs is a no-pressure workout," former Denver Broncos trainer Bob Anderson writes in his authoritative warm-up encyclopedia, *Stretching*. "You do what you can, at your own speed and at your own rhythm."

Anderson notes that stair exercise works many "neglected" muscles in the leg you probably forgot you had. Anderson would have the Broncos do *at least* thirty minutes of stair work. I'm not that hardcore—find your own stair stamina, increasing your time as you become accustomed to doing this exercise.

A. Begin by walking up and down stairs for two minutes if you can. When you return from your walk, pause at the stairs to your home—or any stairs that are convenient, for that matter.

B. Increase your stair sessions according to your comfort level. Doing stairs has aerobic benefits—it surely gets your blood pumping—so the more you do, the better. Concentrate on the flexing of your muscles with each step.

C. If you're up to it, skip a step, taking two at a time. Every step you take adds to your endurance; every double-step, meanwhile, enhances stamina even more.

D. Don't avoid steps in your everyday life—embrace them. Step out of that crowded elevator and try walking up the stairs to your office. If you must, start by taking the elevator halfway up and walk the remaining floors. *Any* stair work counts as good work. You don't have to walk stairs fast. Instead, keep a steady pace and develop your own rhythm; of course, remember to breathe strategically.

If you're capable of doing more stair time than two minutes, great—but don't worry about breaking any world records. Try not to wear yourself out yet, as my BYGS stretch-workout sequence is just beginning. Increase your stair sessions incrementally, pushing your limits gradually each time. Your physical stamina will grow additionally able to handle more intense workouts. It'll be sooner than you think.

The Perfect Back Stretch

Doing this helps warm up the back muscles—your foundation for all physical exercise. Hey, why not?

How Long Should I Do This?

One to two minutes, or more . . .

The back muscles are the core of all physical exercise, so it's no surprise that this exercise is the foundation of my stretch-workout sequence. Think about it: the back is the fulcrum, the nexus of support, for much of what you do. When you exert your arms, shoulders, neck, legs—all get a helping hand, so to speak, from the back muscles. A strong, straight yet relaxed back is essential for no-fall snowboarding.

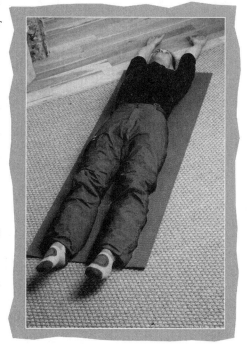

You always want to stretch the biggest, most significant muscles first; remember, the back muscles are the ones helping all the other muscle groups do their job. For example, it's not going to help your neck if you stretch it with a tight back. So let's begin . . .

A. Start the perfect back stretch, by lying flat on the very back in question.

B. Next, stretch both arms over your head as far as you can. Make sure your palms face up to the sky, fingers extended.

C. Take a deep breath in this position, relaxing into the stretch. As you exhale, stretch a little more by pointing your toes and extending your fingers in opposite directions. You're lengthening, elongating your body, as well as stretching the fronts of the lower leg.

D. Take a few more big, deep breaths in this position. Inhale and exhale until you feel relaxed and find the rhythm of breathing. Imagine, as you take in oxygen, that you're sending it through your body to the muscles feeling the pull.

When I'm in this position, reaching with my toes and fingers, I feel my shoulders rise close to the ears. As my shoulders get stretched, I also feel the muscles that connect my back to my shoulders getting a nice, healthy elongation.

A Different Kind of Back Bend

Doing this helps stretch opposing muscles that'll come in handy in the near future.

How Long Should I Do This?
About a minute.

Stay on your back for this stretch, which nicely greases the muscles that link the legs up through the back.

A. Start with a nice, big breath. As you inhale, draw your right knee into your chest.

B. Grab your right knee with both hands.

C. As you exhale, pull your right knee toward your right shoulder. Take another deep breath.

D. As you exhale, try pulling your knee even closer to your right shoulder.

Aaaahh . . . I feel this stretch starting around the back of my knee all the way into the center of my back. It's great for your lower back.

As I stretch, I concentrate on the muscle I'm stretching. As you start to feel it, concentrate on your breathing. Imagine that you are directing oxygen to the place where you feel the stretch. See if the new oxygen allows the muscle to stretch even more.

E. Take another deep breath. As you exhale, extend and lower your leg to the mat. Take a breath in and exhale. *Relax.* Take another breath in. *Exhale.*

F. Repeat the above exercise with the opposite leg. Draw your left knee into your chest; hold the knee with both hands.

G. Take a deep breath. As you exhale, pull your left knee toward your left shoulder.

H. Take another deep breath. As you exhale, pull your knee a little *closer* towards the left shoulder.

I. Take another deep breath. When you exhale, extend and lower the leg to the mat.

J. Take a couple more deep breaths while flat on your back. On your final exhale, bring both knees to your chest: you're now ready to segue into the next position.

Spinal Zap

Doing this helps loosen up the back/spine muscles that help fine tune your balance and motion on a board.

How Long Should I Do This?

Thirty seconds to a minute.

A. You're still on your back, on the mat. Now draw your knees to your chest, keeping the legs together. *Inhale*. As you exhale, grab the knees with both hands. You can even interlock your fingers over those knees.

B. Tuck your chin and rock back and forth along the length of your spine. Take nice deep breaths, inhaling and exhaling.

C. As you rock, take your time; try moving over one vertebra at a time. You're further loosening up the muscles in your back.

D. When this stretch begins to feel more natural, increase your rocking further. Try rocking forward so that you almost (but not quite) come to a seated position. When you rock backwards, see if you can go far enough so the back of your head touches the ground. Spend a minute or two rocking back and forth.

As I increase my rock, I feel my back muscles loosening up. Over time, I've noticed my "rock" has become smoother. This is one stretch you really can't overdo, so if you like it, spend a few minutes or more on it. The more you do this stretch, the better, as it is strengthening and limbering the foundation for all physical exercise.

Sit-Ups

Doing this helps you develop the strength in the "ab" muscles you'll need on your snowboard to get up after sitting down to strap in your bindings, tightening your boot laces, or just resting for a second. All of which you will do. A *lot*. All of which helps build a foundation for that coveted holy-grail of fitness: the almighty *six-pack*.

How Long Should I Do This?
One to five minutes (it depends on how many sit-ups you can do—the more, the merrier).

A. Lie flat on your back, knees bent, soles of your feet flat on the mat. Tuck your chin, then cross your arms across your chest. Ready to do some stomach "crunches"? Take a deep breath.

Tucking the chin in is *important*—this action prevents unnecessary neck strain.

B. As you exhale, try flexing, or tightening, your abdominal muscles. Feel the *crunch?* This curling action in the stomach should raise your shoulders off the mat one, two, maybe even three inches. Hold that abdominal flex for a second, then inhale as you lower yourself back down again.

Try to make sure your shoulders don't rise any higher than three inches off the ground. Raise your shoulders over three inches and you're exercising your hip flexors, not your abs.

Feel that? Now, repeat this three-part sit-up sequence:

1. Exhale, flex abs, raise shoulders
2. Hold
3. Inhale, lower shoulders to floor

Repeat as many times as you feel comfortable.

Day one, the number of sit-ups you're able to do may be minimal: shoot for ten, but even one is enough to get started. As long you increase the number of sit-ups a little every day, in a short period of time these muscles will be strengthened and ready for snowboarding.

The movement you do during sit-ups is repeated every time you get up on a snowboard from a seated position. This is the one movement guaranteed to wear you down and reduce the time you spend on the hill—unless you've prepared your abs.

Your body will tell you if you haven't prepared: you'll be exhausted by the third time you sit up—about ten minutes into a one-hour lesson. Sorry to go on and on about this, but when those muscles stop working, that's when people *fall*.

At the end of your sit-up session, lie yourself down flat on your back. Take a breath. *Exhale*. It's not time to make doughnuts yet—it's time to work the quads.

Once you're good and relaxed, roll over onto onto your stomach. You're now in a perfect position to begin stretching the quadriceps muscles that line the upper front of your leg.

Hot-Rod Your Quads

Doing this helps prepare the muscles needed to bend and lower your body while snowboarding.

How Long Should I Do This?

One to two minutes.

Whenever you bend your knees snowboarding—and that's all the time—the "quads" get exercised. Your quads are the muscles you use to bend your knees and squat down while riding a snowboard, so you can imagine the significance in warming them up.

A. Lie on your mat on your stomach. Relax and put your arms by your sides, palms facing upwards. Take a few breaths.

B. On your final exhale, bend your right knee and reach back for your right foot with your right hand. Pull the right foot down towards your butt. It doesn't matter if you touch your heel to your butt or not.

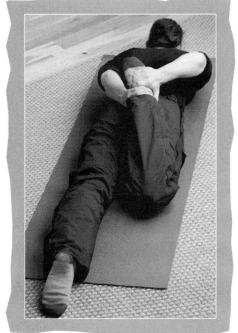

Feels good, doesn't it? Do you feel the stretch along the top of your leg? When you do, relax *into* it. Take a few breaths, sending oxygen to the stretched muscle.

C. On an exhale, reach back with your left hand to grasp the right foot as well. With both hands on the right foot, use your exhale to increase the pull, intensifying the stretch as much as you feel comfortable. You'll *really* feel this in your right quads!

Doing this stretch accomplishes many things: not only have you extended your quads and got blood flowing in the knee joints, you've also given your ankles a good bend.

Lower your right leg and repeat this sequence with the left leg. When you've finished, rest your arms at your sides and relax. Take a breath or two: get all the oxygen you need, because now you're really going to exert yourself. You're in the perfect position for push-ups.

Push-Ups

Doing this helps anyone who needs to stand up from a seated position while strapped to a snowboard.

How Long Should I Do This?

Two seconds to twenty minutes—however long it takes you to do as many push-ups as you're physically capable of.

> **A.** Lie face down on your mat. When you're good to go, sit up on your knees. Next, fan the fingers, placing palms flat and wide alongside your ribs, slightly more than shoulder-width apart.

You might feel a healthy tension in your shoulders here; I always do. Welcome it.

> **B.** Keeping your back straight, take a deep breath. As you exhale, push yourself up and off the ground with your arms.

Not to nag, but remember to keep that back straight.

> **C.** As you rise up, keep your knees and toes on the ground to support your lower body. Once you've extended

your arms to their full length, hold in that position for a breath or two. Inhale as you lower yourself back down.

Because your back is straight, you'll feel some pressure on your knees and hands as they push into the ground—that's good. If you don't keep your back straight, you'll feel more pressure on your toes and know you're not in the right position.

Repeat this sequence as many times as you feel comfortable. Once or twice is enough to start; if you can do ten push-ups the first time around, consider it an achievement. Gradually increase the number of push-ups you do each time you exercise.

There are many ways to do push-ups—this is just one. You can balance on your toes, keeping your legs and back in one long line. If you're a member of our armed services, or were traumatized by a particularly hard-ass gym teacher during childhood, then you know what a "marine" push-up is. These variations simply add more leverage to the muscles, making the push-ups harder and giving your muscles a more intense workout.

Also, if you've had a knee injury, say, or you just don't feel comfortable supporting yourself on your knees, then the toe-balance stance is for you. However, only try the toe-balance push-up if you're familiar with that position already, or after becoming comfortable with the initial stance I've described, supported by your knees and toes. Either variation serves the same function—getting your upper body conditioned for snowboarding.

Push-ups use and enhance the tricep muscles on the back of your upper arm, as well as the chest muscles. Push-ups also provide a great stretch for your wrists—the most vulnerable area affected by a snowboard tumble. The more you stretch your wrists, the less likely you'll injure them in a fall.

The push-up is particularly useful as it mimics exactly the movement used to get up on a snowboard from a seated position. In this common movement, you roll over with the snowboard locked to your feet, into what in wrestling is called the "down position." In the "down position," the toes and knees provide support, with both touching the ground. The palms of the hand, meanwhile, are splayed open wide, with the span between hands a little wider than shoulder distance.

From the "down position," you'll push yourself back onto the toe edge of your snowboard and stand up, ready to ride. Don't be surprised by how quickly all this becomes reflexive instinct. Just a couple hours on snow will be enough to do the trick.

Pushing yourself up from the ground while your feet are attached to a snowboard is very similar to the common push-up most people first learn in elementary-school gym class. However you manage it, this movement truly tones and conditions the upper body. It's okay to take your time—don't be surprised when your few push-ups a day turn into fifty or a hundred. As well, you might notice how little time they use up in your schedule—it's amazing how many push-ups you can pump out in just two minutes.

If you need any further inspiration or guidance, rent the movie *Full Metal Jacket*. They do *a lot* of push-ups in that movie.

Shoulder Initiation

Doing this helps put the power into no-fall snowboarding's power steering.

How Long Should I Do This?

Thirty seconds to a minute for each shoulder—or longer.

For the first standing position in my stretch-workout sequence, I want you to assume what I call my stretching "ready stance."

In order to stretch all the muscles harmoniously, you want to stretch from a neutral, centered position, so that each side gets full benefit. In other words, try to stretch and flex your left and right sides equally.

A. "Ready Stance": stand straight and tall, hands hanging loose by your sides. Relax your shoulders as well, balancing your head directly over your spine. Place feet shoulder distance apart, the outsides of the feet parallel with each other. Bend slightly at the knees. You don't want your knees locked, because then the muscles in your legs aren't working: you're balancing with your skeletal structure, not your muscles, which are just what we're

trying to warm up! The same principle applies to keeping your back straight, too.

B. Take a deep breath. As you exhale, arc your right arm over your head so that your palm faces out, fingers pointing to the sky. At the same time, slide your left hand down the side of your left leg. Stretch that right arm as high as you can.

C. Inhale. On the exhale, lower your right arm and return to the ready position, arms relaxed now at your sides.

D. Next, repeat this sequence, arcing your left arm overhead and reaching down with the right.

E. Keep repeating this sequence until it feels natural. At that point, try raising one arm while simultaneously reaching down with the other. Explore your full range of motion, stretching as high as you can without bending your waist. Repeat the sequence for each arm at least ten times.

We're doing this sequence so many times because this movement translates exactly to

the moves needed for no-fall snowboarding. In *Karate Kid* terms, it's basically the "wax on, wax off" of no-fall snowboarding: you're training your muscles to move exactly as they'll need to move on the slope well before you actually go snowboarding. The shoulders are the steering wheel in no-fall snowboarding, so this sequence is like adding power steering to your body's options package.

The "Off the Wall" Calf Stretch

Doing this helps strengthen the lower legs to turn that snowboard!

How Long Should I Do This?

Thirty seconds per leg.

I can't overemphasize the importance of warming up the calves before snowboarding—in fact, insiders call them the "snowboarding muscles." To initiate a turn, you shift your weight to either your toes or your heels—you're on one or the other all day long. Standing on the toes works not just the feet but especially the backs of your legs. You'll feel your calf muscles snowboarding, believe me, so it's best to be prepared.

A. Assume the "ready stance," but with your back resting against a wall. Make sure your back is flat and straight, with the backs of your heels touching the wall. Make sure you're comfortable and begin strategic breathing.

B. When ready, take a deep breath. As you exhale, bend your knees, sliding your back down along the wall until you feel a stretch in your lower leg.

Make sure your heels remain *flat* on the floor—you don't want your heels to lift off the ground at all. If you find your heels lifting, stop and adjust your position.

C. Hold that position as you take a breath. When you exhale, try re-laxing into the stretch a little deeper. After a breath or two in that position, stand up straight into the ready stance.

D. Then, after a breath, repeat the se-quence, putting a few more nice breaths into those muscles.

Don't worry if you're unable to bend down very far right away. As you practice this stretch, the extent of your range of motion in this area will increase gradually—then *dramatically*.

The Über Upper-Body Stretch, Part One

Doing this helps lubricate your upper body's full range of motion.

How Long Should I Do This?
Thirty seconds per each arm.

Many people tend to concentrate on the lower body when it comes to snowboarding. But in no-fall snowboarding, we ride with the whole body. Everything works together as a balanced unit, so it's important to keep the upper body trained and ready to move to maintain balance. If you do, you're going to be that much better at riding without falling. My upper-body stretch here nicely greases the muscles and connectors in the arms, shoulder and upper back, all of which work together to make the dream of no-fall snowboarding a reality.

A. Assume the ready stance. Stand tall, relaxing the arms at your sides with your feet shoulder width apart. Even out your breathing. Now we're going to give the upper body the stretch it *really* needs to go riding.
B. As your breathing settles into a comfortable groove, make sure the outsides of your feet are parallel with the other.

You may feel that your heels are slightly flared. This is normal.

C. Now, reach your right arm straight across your chest at shoulder height, pointing your fingers to the left.
D. With your left hand, reach over your right arm and grasp your elbow. Take a deep breath.
E. As you exhale, relax your right shoulder while simultaneously pulling your right arm leftwards

across your chest. Pull your right arm as far left as is comfortable and possible. Hold here and breathe.

When I'm in this position, I feel the stretch go from the back of my upper arm and down my rib cage, all along the right perimeter of my body. With your breathing, try to send oxygen to the muscles this stretch is working.

F. Lower your arms to your sides and relax. Now, repeat the same stretch, but with your left arm.

G. When you're done stretching the left side, again, rest your arms at your sides. Relax and breathe.

As you breathe, contemplate what just happened. How did the stretch of your left upper body feel different from your right? You've just given the shoulder, back, and arms an ideal warm-up for exertion on the hill. An ideal warmup *for anything*, I might add.

The Über Upper-Body Stretch, Part Two

Doing this helps further increase upper-body performance on—and off— the slopes.

How Long Should I Do This?
About thirty seconds on each side.

This continuation of my upper-body stretch ensures this area of your body is truly primed and ready to go. And your shoulders will thank you kindly.

A. Stand in the ready position. Now raise your right hand straight over your head. Rotate your right hand so that the palm turns towards your ear, and further so that it faces the wall behind you.

B. Bending at the elbow, reach your right hand down the center of your back.

C. With your left hand, reach over and grab your right elbow. Take a deep breath. As you exhale, reach down the center of your back as far as you can, supporting and increasing the stretch with your left hand on your right elbow.

Feel that stretch in the shoulder, in the arm, and in the center of your back?

D. Now drop your arms to your sides. Relax. *Breathe.*

E. When you feel ready, repeat this stretch sequence from the beginning, but this time stretching the left arm overhead and then reaching back with your left hand.

F. With your right hand grabbing your left elbow, give your left upper body muscles the same journey through their full range of motion that you just gave muscles on your right.

As you build these stretches into your regular routine, you will gradually notice greater flexibility in your shoulders; some notice it right away. Do this stretch sequence every day for a week and see what happens.

The Neck Stretch

Doing this helps turn the neck-shoulder axis into *the* vehicle for total 360 degree vision while snowboarding.

How Long Should I Do This?

Between three and five minutes.

The muscles touched on here are the neck muscles, as well as the muscular group that connects them to the shoulders and the back on both sides of your body. A tight neck is one that's most open to injury and fatigue in snowboarding. Therefore, please consider this sequence crucial in your snowboarding physical warm-up. Be careful to stretch the neck according to my instructions exactly. You won't get much out of rolling and bouncing like a bobble-head doll as some suggest.

Getting the shoulder, back, and neck to work together efficiently is necessary for optimum snowboarding. In addition, you'll find that, the farther you can twist your neck around, the more you can see, resulting in what I call "snowboarding 360-degree vision" (360 dv). A good, safe rider is always aware of what's coming from behind and what's next to her. Enhancing your field of vision like this means there is no snowboarding "blind spot."

A. Now we're going to *really* stretch the neck. We begin as usual in the ready stance, standing with back straight, feet shoulder width apart and arms relaxed at the sides.

B. Looking straight ahead, gently tuck the chin down, with the head balanced directly over the spine.

C. Take a deep breath. As you exhale, *tilt* your head to the right as far as you can. Take another deep breath.

D. On the next exhale, relax your left shoulder, allowing your left hand to slide down the side of your left leg. Inhale and exhale again before returning to the ready stance.

E. Repeat this stretch, but this time tilting your head to the left and reaching your right arm down.

F. Continue this stretch, but modulate it to explore your neck's full range of motion. Start by turning your head *halfway* to your right shoulder. Take a deep breath. As you exhale, tuck your chin in to your right collarbone, bending the knees slightly. Inhale.

G. As you exhale, relax both shoulders, sliding the hands down the sides of the legs. Then, while you *inhale*, stand back up to center.

H. Repeat the same series of movements for your left side of your body. Finish by returning to the centered alignment of the ready stance.

I. Now turn and look as far to the right as you can, so that the chin is as close to edging over the right shoulder as possible. Look behind you as far as you can out of the corner of your right eye. Pick a spot and focus on it as you take another breath.

J. As you exhale, tilt the head back, looking straight up at the ceiling. Take another deep breath.

K. Now as you exhale, relax the shoulders again and slide both hands down the sides of the legs.

L. Inhale, returning to the ready stance. Repeat this sequence for your left side.

Congratulations—you've completed a full neck and shoulder rotation. When I do this stretch, I feel its effect through my whole neck.

The Lower-Body Lowdown

Doing this helps get your shock absorbers ready, baby.

How Long Should I Do This?

Forty seconds to a minute.

Your lower body has few, but important, functions in no-fall snowboarding. Most predominantly, the lower body absorbs terrain: when you bend your knees and ankles, you're increasing and decreasing the pressure of the snowboard on the snow as the snowboard moves over ridges, drifts, and bumps. You can also use the bend in your knees and ankles to adjust the angle of the snowboard to the snow, allowing for more aggressive riding.

The more aggressive your stance—bending the knees as far down as their full range of motion will allow—the more aggressively the snowboard is going to react. This stretch is the perfect way to mark your progress as a snowboarder: the more you're able to stretch the lower body, the more aggressively you'll be able to ride.

A. Begin in the ready stance. Bend the knees slightly and take a deep breath.

B. As you exhale, bend at the waist: letting your arms hang freely in front of you, try reaching for the floor. Take two or three breaths here, as this is an important moment in the warm-up: you're stretching the back of your upper leg, as well as giving the lower back one final warm-up.

This stretch always gives my hamstrings a good elongation. I take a couple extra breaths here because I really want to get oxygen to these muscles; try directing your inhale to the hamstrings on the back of your leg. On the hill, you'll discover why preparing your hamstrings is such a good idea: every time you stand up on a snowboard, your hamstrings get a workout. You'll be standing up *all day*, so get ready.

Squat. A Lot.

Doing this helps get your shock absorbers ready.

How Long Should I Do This?

One to two minutes, or more.

Squatting is cool. Real cool. My squatting method is *extra* cool. It stretches the calves, while at the same time flexing quads, feet, and ankles. Stretches and flexes aren't the same thing. In a stretch, the muscle is relaxed as you elongate it through its fullest range of motion. When a muscle flexes, however, you're actually *using* it, and the muscle tightens. As such, the move described below gets you ready for anything. This squat involves many of the essential muscles used in snowboarding.

My squat proves most excellent for the back of the leg. The calf muscle is crucial for standing on the toes. In snowboarding, you're always on either a toe-side or a heel-side edge—therefore, half the time you ride you're on your toes *alone*. Get those muscles ready before you get to the hill and you'll be able to have fun longer because your muscles won't fail you halfway through the day.

You're flexing quads here, too. Your ankles and feet will limber up as well, and that's good news: they are the closest thing to that snowboard, so they need to be strong and able to move in many different directions. If you're planning on strapping an X-Game vehicle like a snowboard on your feet, you want those muscles primed so that when you hit the hill, you can just let go of the clutch and *go*.

A. Begin in the ready stance. Back straight, take a *deep* breath.
B. As you inhale, bend at the knees. Lower yourself as far as you can while keeping the back straight and the balls of your feet on the ground.
C. As you exhale, stand back up. Repeat the squat movement at least ten times. As you get used to doing the movement, add as many additional squats as you can to your repetitions.

I'm feeling the front of my legs flexing. I'm feeling tightness in my knees, and a stretch in my calves and hamstrings. It's pretty complete: this squat is, in fact, adapted from a great, old-school exercise called the "Zercher squat," developed back in the '30s by renowned St. Louis power lifter Ed Zercher (see "Old School Strength," Jim Stoppani, Ph.D., *Muscle and Fitness*, October 2004, p. 70). Fitness freaks today dig the Zercher squat for its thorough exertion of the glutes, lower back, and legs.

Once you've gotten comfortable with your squats, well, let's get a little crazy. We're going to integrate my squatting exercise with the shoulder movement described in under "Shoulder Initiation," above. This is a little more advanced, so don't worry if you don't get this right off. If you do get it the first time, well . . . Bravo!

The Squat-Shoulder Flex/Stretch Combo

Doing this helps snowboarding, period. This move sums up all the necessary muscles and movements used in no-fall snowboarding.

How Long Should I Do This?

As long as you can; it's the good stuff . . .

A. Begin in the ready stance. Inhale as you bend at the knees and ankles. Keep the back straight as you lower yourself.

B. As you bend the knees, begin raising the right hand—fingers pointing towards to the sky, straight up and palm out—raising the shoulder at the same time.

As my right shoulder is raised along with my hand, I relax my left shoulder even deeper, helping extend my right arm upward in its fullest range of motion.

C. Once you're fully elongated, pause and take a breath. Upon exhale, return to the neutral ready stance.

D. Repeat this movement sequence using the left arm. Do at least ten repetitions on each arm, always returning in between to the ready stance.

Now we're going to pick up the pace and tax your coordination-agility abilities a little; if this proves too much, leave this last bit until your body has built up more endurance after a few complete workouts.

A. Start in the ready stance. Take a deep breath. As you exhale, raise your right hand way above your head, palm facing out.

B. Take another deep breath. As you exhale, point the fingers of your right hand toward the sky while simultaneously relaxing your left shoulder, reaching the left hand down that leg. Let the left shoulder follow the left hand down into a stretch, exploring your full range of motion in this position.

C. This time, as you inhale, simultaneously bend your knees and ankles, lowering yourself down. Keep your back straight and go as low as you can, until you can no longer keep your heels rooted to the ground.

D. Repeat this sequence at least ten times—more if you can. Inhale as you return to the ready stance.

At first, you'll only be able to hold this position, which combines a shoulder-back stretch with a knee-quads flex, for a few seconds as your quads will start to whimper. After snowboarding for sixteen years, however, this movement feels utterly fluid and elastic to me.

Indeed, my range of motion—in all my muscle groups—feels like it's grown exponentially: riding all the time allows my body to work with full flexibility and range of motion. I'm in my forties, and people tell me I move like a teenager.

Best of all, this happened while I was having fun, doing a sport I love so much I made it my occupation. I never really thought about trying to stay in shape; after a while, I just *was* in shape, all the time. It's funny—I'm in the best shape of my life, and I barely noticed it happen.

Aside from its pure benefits as physical fitness, warming up your muscles so they have access to their full range of motion prepares them to move in any direction. If something unexpected happens on that snowboard, your fully stretched and oxygenated muscles are that much more prepared to react. You'll automatically start using movements you've downloaded into the muscle memory. You'll see.

Trust me. If you can't do that yet, then trust how you feel after a week or two doing my stretch-workout sequence regularly. Your new and improved body will practically beg you to strap on that snowboard and take it for a high-energy jam down the mountain. As Bruce Lee himself once said, "We have two arms and two legs. The important thing is, how can we use that—to the *maximum?*"

So shall we get down to it and really learn to snowboard?

Smoothies:
The Non-Wheaties Breakfast of
Champions for Snowboarders

My ultimate smoothie recipe is not about calorie cutting—there's something in here for every diet guru to argue with. I won't guarantee it's going to make you thin. Instead, my smoothie is all about preparing the body for snowboarding.

A good, healthy smoothie provides quick energy—and a quick breakfast that won't take up precious time that could be spent snowboarding. It provides fuel to burn while riding the slopes. Meanwhile, enzymes in the fruit aid digestion. In short, you get lots of good stuff out of the ingredients—proteins, natural carbohydrates, and vitamins (it's chock full of vitamin C). In other words, it's *balanced*. Sound familiar? And did I mention it tastes good?

DANNY'S ULTIMATE SMOOTHIE RECIPE

Ingredients:

1 and a ½ cups yogurt

1 large banana

2 kiwis

1 papaya, or mango, or peach

1 handful of raspberries or strawberries

1 handful of blueberries

1 cup soy milk

1 cup white grape juice

This recipe makes one quart, which fills roughly four glasses to divide among your snowboard buddies. Start by placing the yogurt in to the blender; you can use high or low fat yogurt, depending on your needs and likes. Higher fat content does make it taste better . . .

Follow with the banana, kiwi, papaya, and the various berries (the kiwi is key—kiwis have more vitamin C than most fruits). Fresh fruit is always best, but frozen works well, too. If you don't want to suck down an ultra-cold beverage before hitting the snow, defrost the frozen fruit in the refrigerator overnight.

Fill up the remaining space in the blender with soy milk and grape juice (guava and apple juice make for good sweetening options as well). Be sure to leave at least a half-inch or so at the top of the blender pitcher—it will spill over nastily if too full.

Unlike every other single thing in this book, don't feel like you must follow my recipe exactly. A perfect smoothie blends everything just right, yet like snowflakes, every one is different. Freak out at the health-food store and see what you like. I often add noni juice, liquid vitamins, ginger, or liquid chlorophyll, to name a few good options. Customize your smoothie according to taste, lifestyle, health needs, whatever . . .

And did I mention it tastes good?

Step 3—Get Balanced

> "Here is natural instinct, and here is control. You are to combine the two in harmony . . ."
>
> —*Bruce Lee*

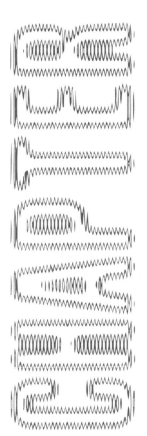

You probably have noticed a preponderance of quotes from Bruce Lee as you pore through this book. My fixation on the wisdom of Bruce Lee is not coincidental, and has everything to do with finding balance in all physical fitness.

In my journey to develop the best way to snowboard, I found myself frequently returning to the lessons of my first martial-arts hero, Bruce Lee—and my martial arts training in general. I've found useful parallels between Bruce, the martial arts, and snowboarding. By the way, I hope you haven't stopped reading if you're not interested in martial arts; ownership of numchucks is not necessary to learn my no-fall snowboarding technique. Not at all, in fact.

What I'm talking about, the parallels between martial arts and snowboarding, is more about the best way to get yourself balanced. In all things. In martial arts, one starts by attaining balance in the body; then balance in one's life and health seems to follow.

That same thing happens when you learn to balance on a snowboard: life follows. Or is it the other way around?

Please allow me to introduce first not the *what* and *how* for my technique, but the *why*. Getting you to understand what's going on in this crucial first step is almost as important as taking that step.

So indulge me.

When it comes to snowboarding, it's best to emulate Switzerland: one wants to start out completely, utterly *neutral*.

At first, neutral doesn't sound very . . . snowboarding: there's nothing "radical" or "extreme" or . . . *sexy* about "neutral." In fact, contrary to what ye olde traditional snowboarding instructor probably told you, neutrality is good when it comes to snowboarding.

Neutrality inherently implies "balanced," and snowboarding correctly is all about balance. This chapter will show you that in no-fall snowboarding, neutrality is the only true foundation on which to build all that is relaxing, extreme, spiritual, sexy, radical, or chill about riding that board down the mountain. Achieving this balance will allow you access to whichever flavor of snowboarding you prefer.

Neutrality in snowboarding is, in fact, one thing I'm decidedly *not* neutral about. What I've discovered in my thirteen-plus years as an instructor is that starting in neutral, in particular The Neutral Balanced Position™, is the first step to achieving total control over your riding. Did you notice the trademark symbol? That's because the Neutral Balanced

Position (hereafter known as the NBP) is trademarked to me. I invented it. I hope you like it.

I discovered the NBP after years of research on balance—and after much tumbling. My butt paid for your snowboarding sins well before you even knew you had any. It's the one time I could maybe say that falling while snowboarding was worth it: I fell, so you don't have to.

The discovery of the NBP was an epiphany. I call what I experienced that day "felt physics": I *felt* the rock-solid stability in a way that convinced me there was no way I was going to fall. I knew it was going to work because I'd never felt so stable, *really* stable, on a snowboard. I felt this stability in my bones, and they thanked me for this change: suddenly I wasn't falling anymore, or overtaxing my skeletal system unnecessarily. I knew it was true when I had an increasingly pain-free bum.

I discovered the NBP around ten years ago, and have been perfecting it ever since. I was working at a big Colorado winter resort at the time, teaching mostly beginners—so many beginners. That's all there were to teach. Ten, sometimes eighteen at a time. Seven days a week. I was on the hill every day, whether I liked it or not. Thankfully, I did.

Interest in snowboarding was growing at such a rapid rate the resort hired seven additional instructors to keep up with demand. Snowboarding was new enough then that not only were most of the people taking snowboarding lessons novices, the people teaching them were kinda novice, too. So was I, considering what I know now, despite the fact that I'd been snowboarding for six years at that point.

Because of the relative newness of the sport, we never stopped creating and re-creating snowboarding conventions, making up the rules as we crashed along. We were excited, and loved what we were doing: my snowboard-instructor peers and I were like a research team. We were constantly redefining anew the idea of what snowboarding was. The mid-'90s was an era of tweaks and valleys for us, the faithful hardcore. We were working through our merry trial of errors to create snowboarding in our image, for better or worse.

Right away I began forging a distinctive style. Because I was teaching so many beginners, I was using a little, skinny Alpine racing board with hard boots, with just the front boot snapped onto the board, riding one foot (the rigidity of the racing boot makes it easier to ride one-footed). Why ride one-footed you ask? Well, in order to walk my students through their turns I had to be able to respond extra quickly: the speed of the racing board can keep you one step ahead of your students. With the one-boot setup I could literally ride circles around them, making razor-quick turns to catch their tumbles.

When I wasn't tumbling myself, that is. I found that rotating my hip to initiate turns—the way I'd been taught to make turns on a snowboard—didn't work while riding one-footed. It would put a lot of twist on that single foot, causing the board to shoot out in front of and cause me to lose balance, which resulted in . . . falling. And *pain*.

Therefore I began to experiment in earnest to perfect my one-footed technique. It got me thinking: If I can figure out a method for better stability on one foot, why not *two?* Why couldn't I ride with ultimate stability all the time?

That's when I figured out my big innovation: snowboarding is about steering with the shoulders, not hips. As I was riding one day, I noticed that, when I raised my shoulder, it would cause me to initiate a turn. Intrigued, I started experimenting with "shoulder steering." When I raised my left shoulder while in motion down the hill, I would turn left; conversely, raising my right shoulder would produce a rightwards drift.

I no longer needed to use my lower body to twist and push through the turns. The best thing to do, I discovered, was to keep everything *neutral*, relaxed, and just let my shoulders do the work. If I did so properly, I discovered it was more efficient to stay neutral; when I "cheated" and forced a turn with a waist twist, or used my foot like a rudder to skid, I immediately felt dangerously unstable. Once I got used to this new shoulder-steering approach, it was actually easier to do it right than the wrong way I had been taught—and had been teaching.

In mind/body disciplines like martial arts and yoga, the talk is always about using the energy from your "center." And when you're bombing down that hill on a snowboard using my no-fall technique, you're working *around* exactly that center—the center is the NBP.

The natural, untrained impulse when you're on a snowboard in motion is to lean back to balance, then try to twist the snowboard in the direction you want to go using your hips and feet. My technique suggests doing the exact opposite. Snowboarding is one area where I've discovered it's best to *not* trust your instincts. I had to train myself to lose the bad habit of using the hips to turn. I had to continually stop my hips from even attempting to turn.

My conversion didn't take long, though. Once you become used to shoulder-turn initiation and the NBP, you get so comfortable being balanced on a snowboard that it becomes natural. Indeed, I was excited about my discovery of the NBP; it made all other methods of teaching snowboarding seem obsolete.

I wanted my students to experience the "felt physics" themselves and avoid having their tailbone bruised as they crash for the tenth time—in just the first lesson. When teaching, I'm always trying to explain to students how to do what they need to do; therefore, I had come up with something as easy to do as it was to understand. In fact, what I discovered was easier done than said for once: it was harder to ride the wrong way once you'd tasted the right way.

The NBP became the foundation for my instruction, giving all my students a stable base from which to learn how to snowboard, figuratively and literally. Anyway, enough with the reminiscing—let's begin the simple, achievable sequence of steps that make up the NBP. First, however, let's figure out if you ride "goofy" or "regular."

Which Foot Forward?

If you thought *Huh?* when I asked if you rode "goofy" or "regular," well, that's understandable. That's snowboarding terminology (borrowed from surfing, naturally) that refers to which foot is in the front binding pointing down the hill.

"Regular" means you ride with your left foot in the front binding; "goofy" refers to riding with your right foot forward. Personally, I don't like these terms—who wants to be called "goofy" just 'cause some surfer thought it was funny? This isn't Disneyland—in my world of no-fall snowboarding, there are no "goofy" people. I prefer the terms "left-foot forward" and "right-foot forward": both are created equal *and* exactly specific to what you'll be doing on a snowboard.

The best way to determine if you ride left-foot or right-foot forward remains accessibly basic:

1. Find a slick-ish ground surface—a wood floor in a gym, perhaps, or maybe a linoleum kitchen floor. Take off your shoes but keep your socks on.

2. Take a few quick steps for momentum, then slide on that slick surface.

3. *Ta-da!* The foot you put forward when you slide is your front foot.

The Right Stance

Once you determine whether you're left-foot or right-foot forward, it's time to assume the Neutral Balanced Position.

The first step: figure out your *stance width*—the distance between your feet when you're locked into your bindings on a snowboard. The Neutral Balanced Position is based on determining your natural snowboarding stance width.

You need to establish the stance width that's best for you, and I mean *you* specifically; it's different for everybody. There's no one "correct" stance, no matter what other books, magazines or your instructor might've told you during that disastrous first snowboarding lesson.

In my system, your stance width is determined by the span that occurs naturally when you walk—your *natural-stride distance*. Because this stance is one you are already used to using, you'll feel comfortable balancing on the board almost immediately. Job one in attaining the NBP is to measure your natural-stride distance, which determines how far apart your feet should be placed on your snowboard.

Step 1: Determining Your Natural-Stride Distance and Stance Width

1. Begin by walking as close to your natural stride as possible—neither dragging your feet like you're headed to the principal's office nor sprinting to the bathroom, but somewhere in between.

2. After ambling along for about ten feet or so, stop suddenly. *Voila!* The distance between your left and right foot is your *natural-stride distance*. That distance is exactly the spacing between your feet on the snowboard itself. In snowboarding jargon, this is known as *stance width*.

There's a reason for matching your natural stride to your snowboard gear setup: you're already comfortable balancing in this position as you walk. If the stance width you use when you strap a snowboard to your feet is exactly the same as your natural-stride distance when walking, the balance you've developed from a lifetime of walking transfers readily to snowboarding.

GOT THEM OL' WIDE-STANCE BLUES AGAIN?

Full disclosure: my use of the natural-stride distance to determine where to place the feet on the snowboard moves in direct contrast to the most trendy stances dominating snowboarding right now. What's cool in snowboarding right now—what looks good in ad photos and movies and sells snowboards—is a super-wide stance width.

Why does a duck-footed wide stance look so cool in photos? It's the snowboard equivalent of the showboating guitar windmills The Who's Pete Townsend became famous for, or how the bass player in The Clash played his instrument hanging down at his knees—even if it actually makes playing harder. In other words, a wide stance is rock and roll, hang-loose fashion that has nothing to do with snowboarding correctly and better—at least the way I ride.

A wide stance looks especially radical when a rider performs tricks of the "jibbing" or "bonk" variety. These are slope-style tricks that frequently use the board to spring in the air and bounce off objects, the rider twisting and turning while balancing to overcome obstacles with style. In one specific type of "jibbing" a rider, strapped on a snowboard, slides down a stair rail in emulation of skateboard tricks. Snowboard companies love jibbing—you don't even need snow to do it, making it a powerful marketing tool to sell snowboards to jib-crazy kids even in, say, Death Valley.

The snowboard powers that be—again, most of them coming from the ski mentality that believes snowboarding is merely a variation of skiing—also think that spreading your legs wide will make you more stable. They are wrong. Do the math: why would anything but the position in which you feel most stable—*walking*—do while snowboarding? Yet the wide stance craze is so intense that some snowboard manufacturers only make boards that start with a twenty-inch stance.

I read recently about a snowboard pro who's just five foot, seven inches tall yet rides a twenty-one inch stance width—a stance better suited to someone eight inches taller. As well, this snowboard pro rides with his boots pointing at exaggerated, duck-footed angles. After a few years of absorbing constant impact while riding such a stance, the guy will destroy his knees. He'll be a hobbled senior citizen—at thirty.

Later on, when I investigated the actual science underpinning this new snowboarding stance, I proved to myself via textbook physics that this was the most stable way to get down a snow-covered mountain. This heightened balance I was experiencing wasn't just in my imagination. The overall lesson learned here is thus: buyer beware—always ride *naturally* balanced.

Step 2: The 51 Percent Solution— Ready, Set . . . Relax.

Once you've figured out the stance width that's right for you, then get ready, get set . . . *relax*.

That's right: relax. First off, in snowboarding, always think relaxed. Jerky, abrupt movements can cause you to catch an edge, resulting in scary tumbles. When relaxed, your body moves with more symmetry from one turn to the next, with your muscles and joints working smoothly and naturally.

Learning to ride relaxed starting from the NBP will train your body how to move from left to right, and from right to left, using the same simple, elegant moves every time. "Relaxed" doesn't mean "passive," though: subtle movements used with the correct positioning will get you where you want to go. Once you're good and relaxed, you're ready to learn where to put your weight, an absolutely crucial element to my technique.

Step 3: Place the Proper Weight on Your Front Foot:

1. First relax your shoulders as much as possible—let them drop. Let your arms hang naturally at your sides.
2. Next, try placing 51 percent of your weight on your front foot (the foot pointing down the hill) by bending your front knee and ankle to shift your weight. This allows your mass to be controlled by subtle, easy movements of the shoulders and upper body.

How does this feel? It should feel as natural as, well . . . Okay, we'll go to the Great Masters for an explanation. If you're near a computer, fire up Google and search for an image of Michelangelo's "David."

Do you see how David balances himself on his back leg, putting slightly more of his weight on that back foot? Artists of the Renaissance called this method of balancing *contrapposto*—according to the glossary at www.christies.com, it's "an Italian term describing the graceful posture of a figure with all the weight balanced on one leg." Try doing it yourself—chances are, you've balanced yourself like this hundreds, thousands, *millions* of times.

Now try balancing yourself with your weight placed more on your *front* foot; this is a basic stance in no-fall snowboarding, and most likely you do it subconsciously a hundred times a day anyway. It feels natural, comfortable, totally balanced, and so will the NBP when you've practiced it enough.

To attain the ultimate balanced starting position, practice these easy steps (start first by standing on the floor; soon you'll be practicing them on a snowboard—first at home, then on real snow). Repeat as necessary.

1. Assume your proper "stance," placing your feet apart.
2. Bend your knees slightly. I call these "soft knees."
3. Pivot on your heels and turn your feet so that your "front" foot is angled the same, or maybe a bit more forward, than the "back" foot.
4. Stand with your hands by your side, then bend your front knee and ankle to place 51 percent of your body weight on your front foot.
5. The front foot can be positioned approximately at a 20 to 45 degree angle, while the back foot may be closer to 0 degrees, or at a right angle to the length of your board. The angles you use will depend on the width of the snowboard you are riding. You want to position your toes and heels as close to the edges of the snowboard as possible, without going over the edge and creating *toe* or *heel drag*. What happens in heel/toe drag is this: if your toe or heel hits the snow, it will pry the snowboard's edge off the snow, resulting in loss of control that can lead to a fall.

Congratulations—you've assumed the proper NBP! But we're not done yet . . .

Step 4—Turn Without Twisting

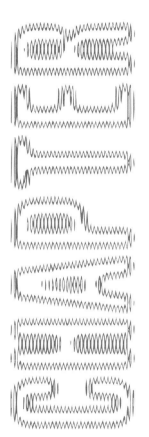

Twisting is the bane of almost any sport you can imagine. Think about all the negative implications of the word "twist"—twisting your ankle, twisting your arm; it's not pretty. Yet twisting is the foundation of the old-school style of snowboard instruction—you're constantly instructed to twist your waist and knees to throw your weight around in order to turn. All that twisting, however, wears the body out and can lead to serious injury. And all that twisting undermines stability. That's why I strove to make my no-fall snowboarding technique twist-free.

Knee and Ankle Bends

Once you can assume and maintain the NBP, it's time to learn how to turn. Here you'll learn not only how to turn without falling or twisting, but also how to control the intensity of the turn.

Here's how:

1. Assume the NBP, relaxing the shoulders, letting arms hang, and placing 51 percent of your weight on your front foot. Then place hands on hips. Keeping the back straight, practice lowering and raising the center of your body by bending your knees and ankles.

2. The amount of bend in your knees and ankles determines your speed and acceleration—think of them as your personal snowboarding gas pedal.

3. Make sure that you are not bending at the waist or twisting your hips, knees, ankles, or feet to balance or increase speed. In slow and precise movements, raise and lower your balanced center by bending at the knees and ankles. Explore your full range of motion. Practice these movements until they become smooth and fluid as you remain balanced.

Even the smallest of these movements will have an effect on your snowboarding. By employing these movements in different increments, a snowboarder will be able to make large to small turns, increase and decrease the pressure of the snowboard to the terrain, and ride more or less aggressively.

The Shoulders: No-Fall Snowboarding's Steering Wheel

Now try combining the NBP with my patented shoulder-steering movements. It's this combination of movements that will cause you to turn effectively on a snowboard.

1. Begin by assuming the NBP.

2. Slowly raise your right arm to the side until it is pointing up. As you raise the right arm, lower the other commensurately, dropping the shoulder as you do. Make sure that you are not bending at the waist, or twisting your hips, knees, ankles, or feet. Repeat this exercise with the left arm.

3. As you rehearse this exercise, observe how your shoulders move—how one rises as the other lowers,

like a see-saw. Repeat this movement until it becomes smooth, fluid, and natural.

4. Practice slow and precise movements, raising one arm as high as you can while lowering the other to your side at the same time.

5. Experiment with small and large movements, stopping and starting at different points. Note how your body and balance feels as you explore different positions and speeds.

6. Try raising your shoulders while keeping your arms relaxed at your sides. In fact, try raising your left shoulder while you lower your right shoulder, sliding your hands up and down your sides. Again, practice these movements slowly and precisely, raising one shoulder as high as you can while lowering the other simultaneously.

7. Explore your full range of motion by elongating your shoulder fully as you raise it up. Make movements of varying size, stopping and starting at different points. Make sure you're not twisting. Isolate this movement until it becomes smooth and fluid.

8. Now raise your right shoulder while lowering your left shoulder, all with your arms relaxed at your sides. Practice this movement until it feels natural.

These movements that you are practicing can be both subtle and aggressive: remember, even the smallest shift will affect your snowboarding. Making this sequence of movements instinctual will give you maximum control.

Look Anywhere Without Falling— Or Changing Direction

Using the Neutral Balanced Position also allows you to look anywhere without changing direction; that's in direct contrast to typical snowboarding instruction, which states that where you direct your gaze is where you'll steer your board.

While it's good to look in the direction you're heading, it's *safer* to be able to turn your head and look anywhere, at any time. This allows you to see in all directions whenever necessary, giving you more control and agility. In short, it's easier to *prevent* accidents. In the "old way" of snowboarding, if something—a crash, a scream, thunder, someone calling your name, a cute boy, girl, or bear—causes you to turn your head suddenly, it doesn't make sense that your whole body should be thrown out of balance as a result, exposing you and those around you to increased danger. But that's just what can happen.

You can master this long before you hit the mountain. You'll feel it when it's right. So, are you ready to start snowboarding for real *without* falling?

No-Fall Snowboarding at Home

"You have to train. You have to keep your reflexes so that when you want it, it's *there*."
—Bruce Lee

Getting used to being strapped to a snowboard is a key element in learn-ing the sport. For many, especially those who have never learned to, say, ski or skateboard, strapping both feet to a moving plank can feel . . . *exotic*.

The more you can familiarize yourself with the feel of your boots and bindings, the better—they are your suspension, your clutch, *and* your ig-nition on a snowboard. But you can also practice, learn, and absorb every essential movement used in no-fall snowboarding before you ever touch the waxy bottom of your board to the snow. This chapter will describe how to do it in easy-to-follow detail.

I've designed these exercises to be practiced in the comfort and pri-vacy of your own home, or any place of your choosing. Remember that jail scenario Master Holland spoke of? Yes, you could even do them in a jail cell.

It's true: utilizing just your snowboard, bindings, boots and a pillow (uh-huh, a *pillow*), you can, in any environment, thoroughly familiarize yourself with and refine the no-fall snowboarding essentials that I've de-scribed in the preceding pages. If you can absorb the basics of no-fall snowboarding *before* you actually go snowboarding, you'll be that much more advanced and ready to start using the technique once you're on the hill.

If you're planning a snowboard trip, consider renting a snowboard to practice the no-fall home sequence from a shop near your home a couple of days before you leave. Just this small amount of effort will hotwire your body to best anticipate the unexpected on the hill.

It will demystify the entire process of learning to snowboard that much more, too: commensurate with your advance preparation, your skill progression will increase more swiftly. The result? You'll have more quality mountain time to actually *ride*.

Safety note: as you will be strapped into the bindings during these exercises, make sure you practice in a wide, open space—the middle of your living room, perhaps. Strapping in like this can feel disorientingly unfamiliar at first, for both you and your snowboard, which wasn't designed for non-snow use. Therefore, take proper precautions if you are a beginner.

In the event you might lose balance while strapped in, please be prepared: perhaps enlist a friend to spot you through these exercises, or scatter pillows around the practice area. Consider wearing protective gear, like wristguards—the kind one might wear while, say, in-line skating or actually snowboarding.

Increase the Pressure, Increase the Angle: Bending the Lower Body on a Snowboard

1. Once you're ensconced in a place spacious enough to strap in and move around, place your snowboard in the middle of the floor.

2. Next, place a pillow under the front nose of the snowboard.

3. Put on your snowboard boots and strap yourself into the bindings.

For the correct way to set up your bindings and proper stance on the snowboard yourself, or for how to instruct a technician at a snowboard shop to set up your board correctly according to no-fall snowboarding specs, see "The Goods: An Opinionated List of Everything You (And I) Would Ever Need to Go Snowboarding" at the back of this book.

4. Stand up and align the center of your body with the center of the board. After assuming the NBP, let your hands relax by your side.

5. Keeping your back straight, lower the center of your body by bending your knees and ankles.

This movement should be second nature as you've practiced it in both my no-fall workout and in the exercises described in this chapter. As with the workout, when doing this motion, make sure that you are not bending at the waist—nor twisting hips, knees, ankles, or feet.

6. Practice, with slow and precise movements, raising and lowering your center toward and away from the center line on the snowboard. Explore your full range of motion; try stopping and starting at different points in your range, feeling how each movement affects how the snowboard reacts. Keep practicing this movement until it becomes smooth and fluid. As you will experience yourself, even the smallest of these lower-body movements can affect your snowboarding.

Using these exact movements, snowboarders are able to make larger or smaller turns by increasing and decreasing the pressure of the snowboard to the terrain. This controls how aggressively you ride.

Knee and ankle bends raise and lower the center of your body. Practicing them is crucial to teaching your body how to move in the proper sequence to maintain total balance while snowboarding. As well, it strengthens the muscles necessary to hold any position in your full range of motion, giving you the greatest possible control on the snowboard. This action provides the movement and prepares the muscles that allow you to ride more aggressively.

Now, it's time to practice turning on a snowboard in the comfort of your own pad, snow be damned.

Practicing No-Fall Toe-Side Turns at Home: The Easiest Way

1. To learn the sequence necessary in snowboarding to make toe-side turns, begin by standing in the NBP while strapped in to your snowboard, a pillow placed under the front end.
2. Once positioned and balanced, begin raising your back shoulder while simultaneously lowering the front shoulder.

These movements combined will shift you to the toe-side edge of the snowboard; when you're actually riding on snow, doing this sequence will enable you to make a toe-side turn. Combining these shoulder movements with your knee and ankle movements determines the shape or size of the desired turn. Notice how making these movements more aggressively causes the snowboard to tilt on the pillow. Doing this same, exact sequence on snow results in sharper turns. In other words, turning-wise you get what you give when exploring your full range of motion.

Heel-Side Turns: I'll Bet You've Figured This One Out Already

1. To turn to your heel side, begin in the NBP while standing on the pillow-resting snowboard. Raise your front shoulder while lowering your back shoulder.

   This movement will shift you to the *heel-side* edge of the snowboard, enabling you to turn in that direction. Again, remember that combining these shoulder movements with knee and ankle movements determines the intensity of the desired turn; how aggressively you make these moves affects the sharpness of your "turns" here.

2. To become as comfortable as possible with this sequence, experiment with different degrees of turning sharpness. Start by using large shoulder movements to feel the changes in weight pressure between your heels and toes.

3. Next, gradually make smaller and smaller movements until you can feel the smallest shift of weight between your heels and toes. Combine these movements with a knee and ankle bend, exploring the full range of motion in your lower body.

So that's it—the total sequence of movements you'll need to know when you're actually learning to snowboard on the mountain itself. Now you're conditioned perfectly to enact my no-fall technique whenever and wherever you choose. It's your body's best prep for when you start snowboarding on pillows of snow, not pillows of down feathers—a great cram session for the real thing on the slopes.

In fact, those are the exact same movements that I myself use everyday to ride, and the ones that I teach my students in actual on-mountain lessons. You'll learn even more about what this all means in the ensuing chapters, where I put my technique to the test both on real snow and with real science.

Step 5—Use the Method on the Mountain

> "The complex and many faceted only confuses me, and I must search for unity. I have discovered that it is enough when a single note is beautifully played. . . . So I work with very few elements, with one voice."
>
> *—Arvo Pärt*

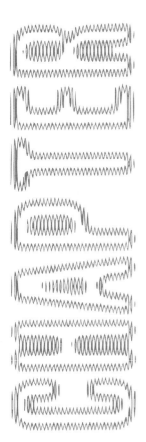

Arvo Pärt is a great modern classical composer of Estonian nationality. He is famous for an innovative harmonic approach which results in haunting, mysterious harmonies atypical of Western music tradition. Iconoclasts like Pärt inspire me: while he breaks with tradition, he still strives for harmony—and that's exactly what I do in my no-fall snowboarding method. I'm breaking with tradition so that when you get on the mountain, you ride in the most simple, harmonious way possible, with every muscle and movement working together to keep you balanced.

In this chapter, my goal is to teach you how to move as if the snowboard was an organic part of you. When you strap that snowboard to your feet, that's the moment you become a snowboarder. I figure you might as well start snowboarding right away—*that's* what this book is about.

To get there, practice and discipline are essential. There are but a few basic moves in no-fall snowboarding; even I find myself constantly refining and perfecting them. With every passing year, I try to make these habits more ingrained, smoother, more instinctual.

My method, as with my stretch-flex snowboarding workout, is designed so that you can practice and, above all, *learn* these movements at home or wherever—all before you head to the mountain. Surprisingly, you'll find it's really not that hard. The words and images here pinpoint and demonstrate *exactly* the balancing and controlling movements in my no-fall snowboarding technique.

The Problem with Ski-Snowboard Hybrids

It's not too often you'll hear the word "exactly" out of a snowboard instructor's mouth. Chances are, if you take four separate snowboard lessons from four instructors, you'll hear four different ways to snowboard. Falling's the one constant to expect from all of them.

One snowboard manual, *Basic Essentials™: Snowboarding* by John McMullen, even goes so far as to suggest not only that "learning how to fall is [an] important aspect of snowboarding," but that "you might actually have to *jump* into the fall" (my emphasis). Well, sure, I used to jump off the roof of my family's garage when I was a kid, too, but just because it was *possible* didn't make it the brightest idea. I wouldn't suggest "jumping into a fall" at fifteen to twenty miles an hour on a snowboard for even an irrepressible impact stunt masochist like Jackie Chan or Johnny Knoxville, let alone one of my students.

Another supposedly authoritative source on the subject, the American Academy of Family Physicians, suggests on their website that the snowboarding novice learn to balance with ski poles! Trust me—don't. You'll most likely get laughed off the mountain. It's like trying to steer your motorcycle with rowboat oars. The AAFP seems to understand this on some level when they recommend that students "learn how to use ski poles from a teacher who knows this technique, because snowboards are not actually designed to be used with ski poles." I agree wholeheartedly with the latter half of this sentence. Ski poles are not for snowboarding— they are for skiing, which is an entirely different sport.

This misguided approach beautifully illustrates the problem with conventional snowboarding methods. They posit snowboarding as a mere variation on skiing—that it's basically skiing with two feet strapped to one ski. A typical aspect of this strange hybrid approach instructs the snowboarder to turn the body square to the fall line and expect the rest of his and her body to compensate for the maneuver. That might get you down the mountain, but not necessarily in one piece. If you're going to snowboard like that, maybe you do need ski poles after all.

Other than a lecture about how you're going to fall, the only consistent thing you'll notice from instructor to instructor is that each lesson will inevitably include some nonsense about "developing your own style." This rhetoric is frequently backed up by some arbitrary, pseudo bio-scientific rationale. One of my favorites is the knee-to-heel rule, which suggests the distance from the knee to the heel is equal to the rider's ideal stance width!

How do I know this is pseudo-science? Well, recently I met with David Lind, professor emeritus of physics at the University of Colorado at Boulder, an expert on snow-sports physics and co-author of *The Physics of Skiing*.

I contacted Lind to find out how well my technique held up when tested against true scientific principles and laws. Of course, I had to explain how my no-fall method is different from how snowboarding is typically taught, so I brought up the ye olde "knee-to-heel" rule. I was surprised by his reaction: he didn't seem like a man given to sudden bursts of emotion, but when I explained the knee-to-heel rule, Lind just started laughing. "Oh, that's not based on . . . anything," Lind chuckled, a dismissive wave of the hand making clear once and for all that the knee-to-heel rule had nothing to do with the laws of physics. (For more of my meeting with Professor Lind and the scientific basis behind my no-fall technique, see Chapter 9, "The Physics—and Metaphysics—Behind No-Fall Snowboarding.")

Physics or no physics, snowboarding isn't rocket science: I've found almost anyone can learn to snowboard fairly quickly when shown the proper techniques. But building confidence on a snowboard is perhaps the most important element to learning.

Most people don't travel down inclines with both feet strapped to a waxed-up plank every day, so that's why learning the basics and getting as comfortable as possible before you arrive at the snow is so important. Soon, what seemed unnatural will become second nature, with you truly taking control of your body's potential.

If you are an experienced rider or skier, you may have to *unlearn* some of what I consider bad snowboarding habits. (See Chapter 10, "Calling All Old Dogs . . .") My favorite students, in fact, are often those who have never even tried snowboarding, or have had maybe a lesson or two but never quite got it.

The biggest difference between my method and the ski-snowboard hybrid approach is that in the conventional way, you're balancing more skeletally rather than using the muscles around the bones. With no-fall snowboarding's movements, you're training your *muscular* system to balance, which allows you to react much faster. You'll feel more confident, with new control. Learning to use these balancing and controlling moves before strapping in for real will give you a solid foundation before you take that first lift—and allow you to maximize precious time on the mountain.

The sooner you absorb these basic techniques, the quicker you'll be getting the most out of your riding. In fact, if you've been doing what the text has told you all along, it's probably already second nature.

So shall we begin, already? To get there, I've divided this chapter into sections that deal individually with essential snowboarding skills while demonstrating and building on how they interconnect. At first, it all may seem like a lot to learn, but it's really not.

Never fear—what you need to remember most when learning to snowboard is this: the center of your body is the fulcrum for your moves. Moving *around* the center of your body's vertical axis allows you to achieve balance and control, as well as your desired speed and direction. Good snowboarding starts from this principle, as will become clear as you make your way through my manual—and down the slopes!

By the way, this chapter outlines the exact routine I myself would take a student through from start to finish at the mountain—it's how I spend my every working day. It's as if I'm right there with you, holding your hand through each element of my no-fall technique.

The "OTM"
(On-the-Mountain) Workout

Being the Zen hard-ass patterned after Master Holland that I am, it's time for—yes—another stretch-flex workout. This time, however, it's adapted to be done on the hill.

I can't stress enough how important it is to prepare your body on the days you're actually snowboarding. Doing my OTM workout could prevent you from, say, tearing a ligament, or spraining a wrist; thanks to increased performance, it can extend your riding day, allowing you to get the most out of your time on the mountain.

WALKING

Walk to the lift in your snowboard boots—that's your warm-up. Walking around, carrying your snowboard, getting yourself ready to go snowboarding, walking to get a cup of hot cocoa with your boots on—all that helps to get the blood flowing. That hot cocoa is an important step. Hot cocoa is the snowboarder's orange juice: when heated, cocoa releases more antioxidants than any other drink.

STAIRS AND CALVES

On your way to the lift, when you get to a flight of stairs, stretch the calves.

A. Stand with both feet on the bottom step, your arm holding on to the railing.

B. Move your left foot back until the ball of your foot rests on the edge of the step. Allow the heel to drop below the level of the step

C. Keeping your left leg straight, take a few breaths, relaxing more into the stretch with each exhale.

D. Repeat with your right leg, breathing strategically.

Your calves are going to be continually working while snowboarding, so you're going to want to do this stretch periodically throughout the day. Anytime you get a chance you should be stretching *something* to keep your muscles warm and limber. After a while, you'll be stretching subconsciously. Listen to your muscles, too—they'll tell you when they need a stretch!

THE CHAIRLIFT STRETCH-FLEX SEQUENCE

I've found that the chairlift ride is a good time to stretch the upper body. A ride typically takes anywhere from ten to thirty minutes; this sequence can certainly be achieved during this time.

Chairlift Workout, Part 1: The Upper Body

A. Interlock your fingers with your palms facing out, straightening your arms out in front of you. You'll feel the stretch in your arms and upper back. Relax into the stretch with a few deep breaths.

B. Keeping your fingers interlocked, move your hands above your head. Sit tall, pushing your palms to the sky. Take some deep breaths in this position. Here we're stretching the arms and upper sides of the body.

C. Next, keeping your arms straight overhead, move your hands as far as you can to the left.

After a few breaths, repeat this movement again, but this time going to the right. This move stretches the left arm, shoulder, and side. Feel it?

D. Keeping the fingers interlocked, next place your hands behind your head, elbows out to the sides. Squeeze your shoulder blades together while taking a few controlled breaths. This stretch gives your upper back, chest, and shoulder blades a good tweaking.

E. Next, unlock your fingers and bend your right arm at the elbow. Grab your elbow with your left hand and pull it towards your left shoulder; this should gently push the right hand down your spine. You should feel an easy stretch in the upper arm and shoulder here. When finished, reverse the procedure, repeating the entire sequence with the other arm.

F. Now we're going to elongate the arms and shoulders through their full range of motion. Grab your left elbow with your right hand, gently pulling your arm straight across your chest. Repeat this movement with the other arm.

Chairlift Workout, Part 2: The Neck

Next up is a neck stretch, which will not only help prevent injury but also prepare you so that you are limber enough to look *in all directions, as far as you can* while you ride.

A. To start your neck stretch, sit up tall in the chair, resting your head squarely on top of the shoulders.

B. Take a breath: as you exhale, tilt your head sideways as far to the right as you can.

C. After two or three breaths, repeat on the other side.

D. Next, return to the position you began the stretch in. Breathe; then as you exhale, turn your head so that you are looking at a 45 degree angle roughly halfway to your right shoulder. Take a deep breath in this position.

E. As you exhale, tilt your head forward, tucking your chin to your collarbone.

F. After holding with a breath or two, repeat this sequence on the other side. This stretches the back of the neck and the upper back simultaneously.

G. From this sequence's starting position, turn your head as far left as you can so that it's in line with your shoulder. Take a deep breath.

H. As you exhale, point chin straight up to the sky.

I. After holding this position for a breath or two, repeat this sequence on the other side.

J. Starting from the beginning position, turn your head as far to the left as you can so that you are looking behind you, over your shoulder. Take a deep breath.

K. As you exhale, try to try to see as far as you can by looking out of the corner of your left eye. Pick a spot behind you and identify it; when you do the same stretch turning to the right, try to locate that spot again.

L. After holding for two or three breaths, return to the starting position and repeat the stretch on the opposite side.

Whenever you practice this stretch, try to see just a little bit more in your peripheral vision. All the while you're expanding your vision capacity in this position, you're simultaneously stretching the back of the neck and upper back, too.

The Final Chairlift Exercise: The Shoulders

To finish up, roll your shoulders forwards and backwards in a circle, breathing deep and slowly.

After four or five rotations, you're finished; now you can really enjoy the view for a moment. . . . That is, until we reach the summit, where we're going to continue my OTM stretch-flex workout.

STRETCH-FLEXING AT THE TOP OF THE MOUNTAIN

Nope, we're not done yet—we've still got to stretch the legs and lower body. And where better to do it than at the top of the mountain?

First, get off the lift at the top of the run (which you'll learn how to do safely *and* easily soon enough).

THE ON-HILL HAMSTRING ETC. EXTEND-O-RAMA

A. Find a comfortable, open out-of-the-way spot to continue the OTM stretch-flex workout.

B. Once you're situated, stand with front foot still strapped in the front binding. Step back with your free foot to kneel on the ground while keeping your front leg straight. Important: make sure you don't bend or twist the knee on your front leg.

C. In this position, take a deep breath. As you exhale, bend at the waist: move your chest toward the knee of your outstretched leg. Take a few breaths here, relaxing the muscles into the stretch, breathing oxygen to them as they work. You should be feeling a stretch in the hamstring and groin of that leg.

D. Now, while still kneeling on the back leg, bend the front knee, too, rocking the snowboard up on its heel edge. Make sure your knee doesn't go past your toes!

E. At this point, place both hands on your front knee. Take a deep breath. As you exhale, push into the knee with both hands. Take a few full breaths in this position.

Feel that stretch? It's a complete one: you should be feeling it in the quads, groin, hips, knee and hamstrings of your front leg.

F. To reverse this stretch, you need to stand back up and step over the snowboard with your free foot.

G. Extend your free foot and bend at the knee, all while kneeling on the ground with the leg that's still strapped in.

H. Put your hands on the free leg's knee, taking a deep breath. Upon exhale, push the knee forward; make sure not to push it past the toes.

I. Take a few breaths here, relaxing into the stretch, sending oxygen to the exerted muscles.

THE SLOPESIDE ULTRA CHEST BOW

The chest bow is an *über*-great hamstring stretch, as I'm sure you'll be experiencing soon.

A. When you're ready, alter your position by straightening the front, unstrapped leg.

B. Take a breath; upon exhale, dip your chest as far as you can towards the outstretched leg. Hold with a few healthy inhales and exhales.

THE BIG MOUNTAIN WAIST BEND

A. Stand up again. Take a breath; bend knees slightly with inhale.

B. Upon exhale, bend down at the waist, reaching with hands as far toward the ground as you can. Take a few breaths, sending oxygen to outstretched muscles.

This movement additionally works the hamstrings and lower back. It will aid you in snowboarding every time you bend to lace your boots or strap down bindings.

To that end, always keep the exercises of this on-hill stretch-flex workout in the back of your mind: it's good to keep the muscles stretched and warm all the time when snowboarding, so consider doing a stretch or two whenever you pause during your riding. Believe me, you'll be stretching like this every time you bend over to retie your boots or adjust your binding strap.

Anyway, enough talk. *Now* you're ready to embrace the glide, so let's go . . .

Embrace the Glide

In your garden-variety snowboard lesson, the first thing you might learn is how to "sideslip" and do a movement called "falling leaf." Think about it—what direction is a "falling leaf" going? That leaf is falling, *brah*. Don't let that be you. Suffice it to say, I don't consider either "falling leaf" or "sideslipping" true snowboarding, but mere skidding, and unstable skidding at that. Snowboard instructors teach these movements as emergency cure-alls in case you run into terrain or pitch that you find intimidating for whatever reason; in theory you can take them at a slower pace while sideslipping. I think you'll find my no-fall method better for tackling tough terrain than the inherently unstable "falling leaf."

Being taught "falling leaf" can take at least an hour, and it's unnecessarily exhausting: typically one's body has had enough after that. To my mind, doing a falling leaf down a tough run will merely burn out the quad muscles ultra quickly—and it's not any fun. I mean, let's dwell for a moment on the operative word in the phrase "falling leaf": *falling*.

Oh, that again . . . Remember, my no-fall snowboarding is organic: I don't believe in unnecessary additives, especially ones that can result in a literal pain in the ass. That's why the very first thing I want to impart my students is not "falling leaf" or whatever the *skid du jour* is. I want my students to learn right away how to move correctly on a snowboard with movements they'll use in *all* aspects of riding.

First I teach the beginner rider how to *walk* and manipulate the snowboard with just the front foot strapped in. Next on the syllabus is learning how to *skate* on the snowboard, pushing yourself into motion with your free back foot. Then I bring those movements together in *straight-*

gliding—that is, moving in a straight line while standing on the snowboard in the Neutral Balanced Position (NBP). Here, you're moving in a straight line down the mountain.

Straight-gliding is especially important to learn right away. For one, you'll need to straight-glide to get on and off the lift safely; two, straight-gliding is the foundation for making turns. If you can't figure out how to go in a straight line, you most likely aren't ready to turn yet. To get you ready to go there, let's start with walking while strapped in.

Walking, Skating and Straight-Gliding in the NBP

You have to learn to walk before you learn to ride—that's my take on that cliché, anyway. Straight-gliding is the "walking" of snowboarding, so it's essential to master it early. As a snowboarder, straight-gliding is the default way to move on terrain that's not good for strapping in—flats, the lift line, getting on and getting off the chairlift.

To get there, though, you must learn how to actually *walk* while strapped to a snowboard with one foot.

ONE SMALL STEP

There are things one must do on a snowboard that don't involve snowboarding, like, say, *walking*—I call all such things "essential non-snowboarding activity on a snowboard."

I like to do as little non-snowboarding activity as possible, but sometimes you can't avoid it. You need to know how to walk and skate and move with that snowboard on your feet. Therefore, it's best to know how to do it right, get it over with, and get riding as soon as possible.

When you first strap a snowboard to your front foot, it's cumbersome—it's hard knowing how to move like that. The first reaction is often to try to manipulate the board and drag it about, or try to walk normally as if the board wasn't on your foot at all. Ain't gonna happen: that board has its own design that dictates how it's going to move.

From the start, a beginning rider will want to know how that board is going to behave with just one foot attached. These specific movements will show you how best to maneuver in this situation.

Over the Top

1. First, get yourself to a nice, flat area where you have some space.
2. Next, attach your front foot to the snowboard by strapping your boot into the binding, making sure your heel is as far back and secure as possible.
3. Tighten your straps until you feel a snug, secure pressure—not so tight that you feel your feet are going to fall asleep, though. You'll be adjusting the tightness and looseness of your bindings off and on all day.
4. With your front foot strapped to the snowboard, put your free back foot behind your front foot, off the board. Make sure your free foot is pointing in the same direction as the one that's attached to the snowboard; this will insure that your body remains in a neutral position.

5. Making sure you don't kick the empty back binding, move your unstrapped back foot over the center of the board and rest it on the ground, putting your weight on it. Make sure the back foot is pointing in the same direction as the strapped-in foot.

Go back and forth, stepping with your free foot over the center of the board and back again, keeping the board flat to the ground. Repeat this movement enough times to make it fluid and comfortable, being careful not to accidentally kick that back binding.

Round in a Circle

1. Return to the position you started in, with your back foot on the ground behind your strapped-in front foot. From this position, move the nose of the board around you in a circle, pivoting on your free back foot.
2. Once you've completed that movement satisfactorily a few times over, step your free back foot over the center of the board.
3. Placing your weight on your free foot, walk the board in a circle, moving the nose around your free foot until this maneuver feels right.

A snowboard when used for anything other than snowboarding is an unwieldy thing, as you now know, but it can be conquered. These movements will teach you how to best maneuver when only your front foot is attached to the snowboard—basically, I want you to get used to the unfamiliar feeling of having one foot locked to the board.

SKATING WITH JUST ONE FOOT IN THE BINDING

Now you can point the nose of the snowboard in any direction you desire while strapped in with one foot. Next, I'm going to teach you how to move in a straight line with your front foot in the binding closest to the board's nose and your back foot unbound and free to maneuver.

This movement is called *skating*, the term taken from its similarity to skateboarding: when you "skate" on a snowboard, you're moving with front foot attached to the board, pushing yourself along with your free back foot.

Your free foot can push from either side of the board. Eventually, the side of the board where your foot is placed will depend on personal preference or be dictated by what kind of terrain you're riding.

But right now, on flat ground—the kind you'll experience, say, making your way through the lift line—it's most important to skate in a balanced position.

A Little Push

1. Start with your free foot placed on the ground directly in front of the foot that's attached to the board. Keep your back, shoulders, hips, knees, and feet straight: any twist in your body isn't good, and will invariably send the board in that direction.

Make sure both feet are pointing in the same direction. Don't twist your hips and waist so that you are facing the nose of the board. Instead, keep your body facing the same direction as your toes, almost as if you're moving sideways.

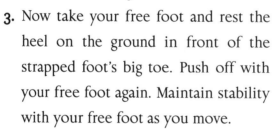

2. With 51 percent of your weight on your front foot, push with your free foot and slide the board in the direction of the nose. This is just a small movement— six inches is *enough*.

3. Now take your free foot and rest the heel on the ground in front of the strapped foot's big toe. Push off with your free foot again. Maintain stability with your free foot as you move.

4. Slowly repeat—*push, slide, step*—until this action feels stable and natural, and you're not kicking your binding each time you bring your free foot up. Take small steps so you don't get caught up in that back binding. This action isn't meant for big speed: skating is simply used to get you from one place to another where you can actually start snowboarding.

Push from Behind

Now let's reverse this skate movement.

1. Place the big toe of the free back foot behind the heel of your strapped-in front foot.
2. Push off to slide the board in the direction of the nose six inches, keeping your free foot stable.
3. Bring your free foot back behind the heel of the front foot and repeat until you feel comfortable with this variation.

Time to Move It

Now that you've taken the necessary preliminary steps, it's time to start *straight-gliding*, the no-fall way.

I recommend starting on terrain that's not too steep: think a slight in-

cline that could be as small as ten yards long. Make sure this area has a flat run-out at the bottom that will allow you to gradually come to a stop without having to brake. Speed freaks, you're going to need to rein in your horsepower for a little while—when first learning to straight-glide, you're not going to go faster than a couple miles an hour. Believe me, at first that will feel fast enough!

STRAIGHT-GLIDING WITH ONE FOOT STRAPPED IN

First I'm going to teach you how to straight-glide with one foot in the binding. This movement is most crucial for getting on and off the lifts, and for traveling short distances that don't have the proper amount of incline to really get going strapped in with both feet.

Riding with one foot can be dangerous if done incorrectly. With just one foot strapped in, you don't even need to fall to twist your knee badly, so be careful, and go slow.

But worry not—I'm going to teach you the exact and proper moves to do this: riding neutral and balanced, using your upper body to tell your board exactly where to go.

1. Stand at the top of a small, gentle incline—one that doesn't have to be accessed by a tow-rope or lift.
2. Next, strap in your front foot. Place the free back foot directly in the center of the board on the stomp pad. Rest that free foot against the front edge of the back binding for stability, giving

yourself as wide a stance as possible without strapping in both feet.

3. Relax your shoulders: let them drop, with arms hanging loose and natural at your sides.

4. Standing as neutral and balanced as possible, shift 51 percent of your weight onto the front foot. *Voila!* You're moving. No, wait, scratch that—you're *snowboarding!*

This position causes you to travel in a straight line: that's because 51 percent of your weight is on that front foot and the rest of you is totally balanced like a gyroscope. Gravity will do the honors, pulling you down the hill.

5. Let gravity direct you down the hill's fall line. At this point, make no adjustment whatever; don't try to steer or lean back. Instead, concentrate solely on maintaining your balance in this position while in motion.

6. As you ride through the run, allow the increasing flatness of the terrain to slow you down and bring you to a complete stop.

7. Take off your board, march up that hill and repeat until you feel *good* about moving this way on a snowboard.

TURNING AND STOPPING WITH ONE FOOT STRAPPED IN

Learning how to turn and stop while straight-gliding on one foot is crucial, especially for getting off the chairlift. On a snowboard, there are three ways to stop your forward progress (well, four if you consider crashing a stop—I don't). One way to stop is by straight-gliding in a straight line until you lose momentum; you can also stop by turning to the left or right.

You want full access to every kind of stop available because you never know when you're going to have to, say, swerve to avoid a dad who's decided to stand right in the middle of the lift's off-ramp to adjust his daughter's glove. Or maybe someone in your way has fallen and can't get up, just like in those old Lifecall medical alert commercials. Humor aside, odds are there's going to be someone standing directly in your path as you're trying to get away from that lift before it dumps someone else on your tail, so you're going to want to know how to get out of people's way as quickly and efficiently as possible!

To that end, it's time to learn *heel-side* and *toe-side* turns. By the way, I've found one of the most confusing things about learning snowboarding is figuring out how "right" and "left" correspond to *heel-side* and *toe-side* turns. That's because each differs depending on how you ride.

If you ride left-foot forward (or "regular"), then your heelside turn tends in the leftwards direction, with your toe-side turn going right. If you ride right-foot forward (the unfortunately termed "goofy"), it's the exact opposite: your heel-side turn angles right, while the toe-side heads left.

Whew, that was tough! I still find that confusing. To clear it all up once and for all so that you *feel* it, first let's start with a *heel-side turn*.

THE STRAIGHT-GLIDE HEEL-SIDE TURN

1. To begin, stand on your board as neutral and balanced as possible with just the front foot strapped in, the free foot resting against the front edge of the back binding. Place 51 percent of your weight onto the front foot to begin a straight-glide run down the incline.

2. As you start to glide, raise your "front" shoulder (the one pointing *downhill*) while simultaneously lowering your back shoulder. This will initiate a *heel-side* turn. This movement will naturally cause you to put more weight on your heel-side edge, causing it to turn in the direction of your raised shoulder.

3. Ride out the momentum of the turn into the flatter part of the run until you stop.

4. You must become comfortable with these subtle maneuvers on flattish terrain before strapping in and tackling the steeper stuff. Therefore, practice as much as you need until you feel agile and fluid making this turn and stop.

Next, step off your board and skate yourself uphill to the top of the incline. Now we're going to learn how to effect a *toe-side turn* while straight-gliding with one foot strapped in. This should prove easy—it's simply a reverse of what you've just done!

THE STRAIGHT-GLIDE TOE-SIDE TURN

1. Standing as neutral and balanced as possible, take another straight-gliding run down the gentle incline you've been practicing on.

2. When you begin picking up speed, raise your back shoulder (the one pointing *uphill*) while lowering your front shoulder at the same time. This movement causes the toe edge of your board to engage with the snow, initiating a *toe-side* turn.

3. As before, ride out the momentum of the turn into the flatter part of the run until you stop on your toe edge.

CONTROLLING YOUR SPEED

If you don't have the convenience of a flat area to let your momentum run out in while one-foot straight-gliding, you have to manually adjust or halt the momentum yourself. Here's how.

The Toe-Side Straight-Glide

1. As you are moving in a straight-gliding motion, to control the speed move your free back foot so that half of the foot is extended over the front edge, with the heel still on the snowboard resting against the back binding.

2. Keeping your weight on the heel, slowly touch the ground with the *toe* of the back foot. This causes your back foot to serve as a

brake, slowing down the board's momentum. At the same time, the external forces you're exerting cause your foot to act as a rudder, initiating a toe-side turn.

The Heel-Side Straight-Glide

1. This time as you straight-glide down, extend the *heel* of your loose back foot halfway over the board's back edge. Keep the ball of your foot on the stomp pad, resting the side of the foot against the back binding for support.

2. Touch the ground with the heel of your back foot, using it as a brake and rudder. Slow down to initiate a heel-side turn.

Again, remember to attempt such maneuvers at *slow speeds only*—otherwise this can be very dangerous and lead to injury.

STRAIGHT-GLIDING WITH
BOTH FEET STRAPPED IN

After some healthy practice of the previous exercises—take as much time as necessary to get them down—return to the top of the gentle slope you've been riding and prepare yourself: let's start snowboarding for real now, with both feet strapped in.

1. At the top of the incline, sit down and strap your back foot into the back binding. With both feet locked in, stand up with the board pointing down the fall line.

There are two ways to stand up. Sitting on your butt, you can push straight up off the ground with your hands and straighten your legs. Otherwise, you can roll over onto your shoulder; once you're on your hands and knees, push yourself back onto your haunches and stand up.

2. Assume the NBP on the snowboard itself. Remember, keep the feet, knees, hips, shoulders, and back all in a straight line. The knees should be slightly bent and relaxed, and your arms loose by your side. Bend that front knee just a little more, putting 51 percent of your weight on that foot, letting gravity do its thing. You're now snowboarding down the mountain!

3. Ride out the momentum to a stop in the flatter area of the terrain.

I think we should take this moment for some congratulations: I'm guessing that, with all the preparation your body has had in terms of balance and exercise, you might've managed to go down a snow-covered incline without falling! You're a snowboarder now—from minute one in this lesson, you've actually been snowboarding.

Furthermore, you've discovered that straight-gliding alone provides a glorious, transcendental feeling—the first time you glide over the ground in this manner can hit you like a metaphysical loss of virginity. It's shocking, in a good way, to discover that the body is capable of floating so lyrically and powerfully.

Straight-gliding's floating sensation feels so amazing and new, especially if you've never done it before. You might want to just straight-glide all day long. Some people never do anything other than this, but don't stop here—there's a whole lot more to snowboarding, and a lot more mountain, left for you to tackle. Straight-gliding is just the beginning.

Turning in Motion

Now we're going to tackle that which scares so many beginning snowboarders: turning in motion. But worry not—your body has already been trained to do this. The point now is just to get used to making the necessary movements to steer on snow itself and build your confidence. You'll get it in no time; soon enough these turning movements will be so instinctual, you'll be doing them without even thinking about it.

TURNING AND STOPPING IN MOTION WHILE STRAPPED IN: HAPPINESS IS A WELL-EXECUTED HEEL-SIDE TURN

Now it's time to learn how to do a *heel-side turn* in motion and come to a complete stop, all with both feet strapped in. Call me optimistic, but if you've been following along in the book so far, I'm guessing you'll find that you already know how to do this.

1. Begin the run at the top of a gentle incline. Strap both feet into your bindings: once you assume the NBP, begin straight-gliding down the hill.

2. As you glide down the fall line, raise your front shoulder and lower your back shoulder simultaneously. This will tilt your heel-side edge into the snow as you move, initiating your turn.

3. Ride the turn out into a stop.

4. Practice, practice, *practice* until you feel comfortable turning on your heel-side in motion.

TURNING AND STOPPING IN MOTION WHILE STRAPPED-IN, PART 2: THE TERRIFIC TOE-SIDE TURN

Now you know how simple it is to turn on your heel-side. You've probably also figured out that, for the toe-side turn, we're merely going to echo the same movement on the opposite side.

1. Starting in the NBP, to initiate a toe-side turn begin by raising your back shoulder as you straight-glide down the hill. This should put you on the toe-edge of your snowboard, turning it in that direction.
2. Ride out your toe-side turn to a stop. Continue practicing this movement until it's unconscious and flowing.

Linking Turns in Motion: Lookin' for the Ultimate Ride?

The title of this section is a humorous paraphrase of a line in one of my favorite movies, the ultimate ironic action-surf heist epic *Point Break*. *Point Break* is Keanu Reeves's greatest pre-*Matrix* action role, and it also features possibly Patrick Swayze's greatest performance ever as Keanu's villainous, mullet-sporting nemesis Bodhi.

Bodhi is Mr. Extreme, an *über*-macho bank-robbin' rebel surfer dude; his intense refrain throughout *Point Break* is that he's "lookin' for the ultimate ride." I wish Bodhi had talked to me first. He could've just learned to link turns correctly while snowboarding.

Learning to link turns is the ultimate, the feeling of freedom personified. When you are finally able to link turns on a snowboard, you can go anywhere and everywhere there's snow. It's the (almost) final piece in the puzzle.

So shall we liberate ourselves and link some turns on the hill?

TRANSITIONS: LINKING HEEL-SIDE AND TOE-SIDE TURNS

Going from Heel-Side to Toe-Side

To make smooth transitions back and forth between toe-side to heel-side while turning in motion, begin by straight-gliding down the hill.

1. Start initiating a heel-side turn by raising your front shoulder.

2. Right when you feel the board begin to turn, begin raising your back shoulder as you simultaneously lower your front shoulder.

3. As you do this, your position will straighten and you will momentarily assume the NBP as a bridge between your heel-side and toe-side.

4. Then, just as you start pointing straight downhill, your weight will shift from your heel-side edge to your toe-side edge. Continuing to raise your back shoulder and lowering your front shoulder, travel in a toe-side turn across the hill to a stop.

You have now linked turns, which is a major, major, breakthrough in your snowboarding ability. Practice linking heel-side to toe-side turns a lot here—see how many turns you can link in a row before reversing this process in the next stage.

Going from Toe-Side to Heel-Side

1. As you start straight-gliding down the hill, initiate a toe-side turn by raising your back shoulder and lowering your front shoulder until you engage your toe-side edge.

2. Right when you feel the board begin to turn, begin raising your front shoulder as you simultaneously lower your back shoulder.

3. Then, just as you start pointing straight downhill, your weight will shift from your toe-side edge to your heel-side edge. Keeping your front shoulder raised and your back shoulder lowered, travel in a heel-side turn across the hill to a stop.

Now, when you feel ready, it's time to take a real run at the top of the mountain and learn how to traverse.

Traversing: Journeying Across The Mountain

Well, the game is up. You know how to snowboard now, so it would only be fair to let you try out your skills on a real run higher up in the thin air, a run with some pitch, one that needs to be accessed by a chairlift.

That's what we're going to do. But before you can try linking turns on a steeper slope, you do need to learn one more thing: traversing on a snowboard. Here's the fun part—you need to practice on a hill that's steep enough to *traverse* on; that tiny hill at the bottom of the mountain isn't going to do it.

According to the dictionary that came lodged in my computer's hard drive, a *traverse* is "a movement or journey across, over, or through something." See, didn't I tell you earlier in the book snowboarding was all about the journey? Now's your chance to journey across the mountain.

In snowboarding, traversing means you're crossing the fall line—you're going across the hill. On one level, a snowboard traverse is something any snowboarder needs to know for safety above all. Traversing is a crucial part of snowboarding, and important to know before you try linking turns on a run with any real steepness. That's because traversing allows you to take on terrain in a careful and deliberate manner, as carefully and deliberately as you choose.

Traversing allows the rider to control the speed, no matter how extreme the incline. For example, if you end up on a run where the incline is too severe for your skill level, you can traverse through it slowly in order to gain control and maintain momentum.

However, I like traversing because it's one more way to ride the mountain. On the mountain and in life, I've never liked to restrict myself to riding a straight line. Skiers ride straight down the fall-line. On a snowboard, however, I feel like I can make my board go anywhere; if I have the momentum, I can even snowboard *uphill* thirty yards or so.

I choose to ride my snowboard anywhere and everywhere I want—or rather, I know how to ride anywhere and everywhere, and knowing how to traverse is one part of giving me that ability. Traversing allows you to go anywhere on the hill. When you are traversing you are truly learning to *control* the edges of your board. On your first day on the mountain, you're learning how those edges respond to the physical input you give them.

Traversing is a progression in terms of your ability as a snowboarder to read terrain ("reading terrain" will be explored in depth in later chapters). When you traverse, you are riding the mountain, exploring how the terrain feels.

Traversing encompasses both *heel-side* and *toe-side* maneuvers. Each of these takes the snowboarder in a different direction *across* the hill, perpendicular to gravity's fall line. In essence, when traversing you're engaging that edge to ride against gravity.

Like a heel-side turn, a *heel-side traverse* takes the rider in the direction of the front shoulder. For example, if you ride left-foot forward, a heel-side traverse ends with a stop where the mountain is *behind* your back and you're looking downhill at the fall-line.

A *toe-side traverse*, naturally, does the opposite. Traversing on the toe-side sends the board into the direction of your back shoulder. When you come to a complete stop in a toe-side traverse, you're staring *at* the mountain, your *back* to the fall-line.

Get it? Got it? *Good.*

Now let's get on the chairlift, get up on the hill and do some real mountain riding. Let's start with learning to traverse on your heel-side.

HEEL-SIDE TRAVERSING THE NO-FALL SNOWBOARDING WAY

1. Take the chairlift up to the most mellow "green" (ski-resort code for "easiest") run you can find.

Learning to traverse on kinder, gentler terrain is key. When you're learning to traverse, sooner or later you're going to have to link a turn to the other edge. You don't want to have to make that turn on too-steep terrain while you're learning because if you make a mistake, you'll suddenly find yourself bombing down the hill at full speed.

2. Skate from the lift to the lip of the run.
3. Next, sit down to strap both feet into your bindings. Once locked in, stand up on your heel-side edge so that your board lies across the fall line.
4. Assuming the NBP, begin simultaneously raising your front shoulder and lowering your back shoulder, as if initiating a heel-side turn.

5. Without letting the snowboard come to a stop, try to maintain movement in that direction *across the run*.

6. Adjust constantly with your shoulders. When the board starts turning uphill, drop your shoulder and return to the NBP until you start gaining momentum, then raise your shoulder again to maintain the heel-edge carve against the fall-line.

7. Use that tension between going uphill and across to your advantage: you can use the traverse to control your speed, bringing it to a velocity you feel good at. Traverse this way until you slow to a stop.

I'm guessing you're halfway down the mountain at this point. Wherever you are, it's time to attempt a traverse in the other direction—on your *toe side*.

TOE-SIDE TRAVERSING THE NO-FALL SNOWBOARDING WAY

So let's say you're stopped in the middle of the run—hopefully in a clearly visible place where you won't be run over. The next thing that has to happen is a turn linking your heel-side traverse to a toe-side traverse.

At this point, what causes people to fall is impatience: they can't wait to allow the board to find the fall line. You might subconsciously want to try to steer the board with your waist, hips and feet as you feel the pull of gravity quicken the pace. Don't—if you force the board with a lower-body twist to steer it, you'll push that edge right into the snow and catch an edge.

Because you've been traversing on your heel edge, your weight is on your front heel; to make a toe-side traverse, you need to switch 'em up. Here's how:

1. Start in NBP, simultaneously lowering the front shoulder and raising the back shoulder. Doing this will cause your board to find the fall-line and start moving downhill.

2. The *second* the board points straight downhill, your weight will shift to your toe edge, and you will be carried across the hill in a toe-side traverse. To maintain the traverse, constantly adjust and alternate as necessary between the NBP and keeping your back shoulder high, your front shoulder low. Ride across the run, keeping the board from going uphill to a stop by adjusting your shoulders in this way.

3. Alternate heel-side and toe-side traverses all the way down the mountain.

4. Once down at the bottom, get back on the lift and repeat until you feel good about your traverse skills. Make traversing instinctual, gaining total comfort in engaging your edges.

LINKING TURNS ON THE HILL

As you get more comfortable with your traverses on the hill, gradually shorten 'em up so that you only traverse a short distance on either your toe or heel side before switching.

When you feel ready, start turning those traverses into linked heel-side and toe-side turns, just like you did on the bunny hill earlier. At this point, reserve your traverse for when the terrain is too steep for you to turn at your comfort level.

Eventually you'll find there is almost no terrain you can't handle using the no-fall snowboarding method. Soon you'll be leaving in your wake beautifully curled, curvy lines carved in the snow by your edges. This is the essence of snowboarding, and you've now captured it for your own personal use.

Here's a refresher for linking turns on the hill:

1. To begin linking heel side to toe side, snowboard across the hill on your heel edge, raising your front shoulder and lowering your back shoulder.

2. When you are ready to make a turn, raise your back shoulder and lower your front shoulder. As you do this, your snowboard will point downhill, shifting from your heel side to your toe-side edge.

3. Reverse and re-reverse this sequence all the way down the hill.

Riding More Aggressively, No-Fall Style

To ride aggressively and dynamically using my no-fall technique, you need to amp up each sequence of shoulder, ankle, and knee movements through their full range of motion.

In no-fall snowboarding, riding more aggressively—with faster speed and quicker, tighter turns—simply means completing all of the movements I've described so far while exploring the movements' full range of motion. Combining the bending of the knees and ankles in their full range of motion with the raising and lowering of the shoulders in their full range of motion will determine the most aggressive turn on a snowboard.

It's like driving a car. If you want to turn just a little, you simply turn the steering wheel slightly. If you need to turn sharply, you turn the steering wheel as quickly and as far in the direction of the turn as possible. The biggest movements create the most dramatic effect, while the slightest movements produce smaller, more nuanced ones. Steering's the same in no-fall snowboarding.

RAISING AND LOWERING SHOULDERS AS HIGH AS THEY GO

Exploring the full range of motion in the shoulders while steering determines not just which edge you're using, but how aggressively you ride that edge. Raising shoulders as high as you can increases the angle of the snowboard to the snow, resulting in sharper turns. If you decrease the angle, your turn will be less sharp. This is true for turns on both your heel-side and toe-side edge.

BENDING KNEES AND ANKLES THROUGH THEIR FULL RANGE OF MOTION

As you move through a turn, bending your knees and ankles keeps the pressure constant to the terrain and increases the angle of the snowboard to the snow. The more you bend your knees through their full range of motion, the more the snowboard tilts up on its edge; this increases the angle of the snowboard to the snow much more dramatically. The result? The more the angle increases, the tighter the turn.

MAKING QUICK TURNS FROM EDGE TO EDGE

To make the quickest turns from edge to edge entails simultaneously exploring the full range of motion in your shoulders and knees as you turn.

For example, the most aggressive, dramatic turn would involve the rider raising the steering shoulder as *high* as it goes while bending the knees as *low* as they go.

As you ride, see how turns are affected as you explore the gradations of range of motion in your shoulders and lower body.

Riding Backwards: F Is for "Fakie"

So you thought snowboarding forwards was intimidating enough. Well, now try *riding backwards*, or "fakie," as it's known on the hill.

Riding backwards is 50 percent of snowboarding. Having the ability to ride "fakie" is the last arrow you need in your snowboarding quiver to become a complete rider. Can you imagine not being able to back your car up in certain situations? Having "fakie" in your repertoire allows you to make turns in any direction, at any time.

If you're going down the hill and a skier cuts right in front of you, if you can ride fakie, you can switch and ride backwards to avoid being cut off. If there's no possibility of making a front turn, having the skill to make a turn backwards could save you. The best part of all, intimidating though it may seem, riding "fakie" isn't that hard. Here's how:

1. Get on a nice, gradual green run.
2. From the NBP, bend your back knee, shifting your weight from 51 percent on your front foot to 51 percent on your *back foot*. Doing this, you'll feel the pressure shift from your front heel to your back heel.

3. Standing on your back heel, raise your back shoulder while lowering your front shoulder at the same time. The board will seek the fall-line and start to move backwards downhill.

4. Keep your weight on your heel until the board is pointing straight down the hill, directly down the fall-line. At this point you will automatically switch to your toe-side edge, carrying you across the hill. You're now moving in the direction of the turn, but via the tail end of the board, not the front.

5. To switch back and initiate another "fakie" turn, switch up your shoulders: raising the opposite shoulder and keeping your weight on your toe edge, let the board find the fall-line.

6. At this point, you will transfer from your toe side to your heel-side edge. Now you're traversing across the hill, riding "fakie" on your heel-side edge.

7. To return to forward out of the "fakie" position, shift your weight to your front heel by bending your front knee slightly. This will cause your board to make a one-quarter turn back to the fall-line. Now you're riding *frontwards* again.

It's All Downhill from Here

Okay, I've already congratulated you earlier in this chapter. Now it's time, though, for *real* congratulations.

If you have followed all of my instruction to this point, you know how to snowboard. You have taught your body to do something new; you've made movements instinctual that you probably weren't used to making previously. You now have a *skill*. You've been rewired for speed. You have tasted *freedom*. With snowboarding, you've acquired a new lens through which to see the world.

And to see your life. If you're anything like me, I'm guessing you just had a full-on encounter with the sublime; I hope so. Snowboarding is what I do everyday, and now you know why. My life has improved greatly since I've started snowboarding, in both health and spirit.

In fact, I find that I figuratively "fall" less in life since I've become a snowboarder and acquired real balance. Mastering everything I've written here is the first step to a no-fall *life*. If you can do what you just did—that is, get on a plank and ride down a hill without so much as a tumble—then I'll bet you can do anything you put your mind to. Now there's still more to learn—there always is in life, too—but the foundation that you've built is the most stable place to work from here on in.

No More "Catching an Edge"

Making heel-side turns correctly using the movements I've suggested keeps the opposite edge of the snowboard off the ground, preventing it from catching in the snow and causing a wipeout—what's otherwise known as in snowboarding lingo as "catching an edge."

"Catching an edge" is the "fall" in no-fall snowboarding. When you catch an edge, the board stops moving and you fall; in a split second, the earth comes up and hits you harder than you've ever been hit before, even if you're a professional football player. Think about face-planting on a snowboard in the terms of, say, an auto accident: how fast you're moving determines how hard you're going to slam. It can be like doing a belly flop into a pool off the highest dive.

Catching an edge is the bane of the snowboarder; it's what makes people swear they will never try it again after a particularly painful lesson. Regardless of whether you're doing a heel-side or toe-side turn, if you maintain the NBP and keep your shoulder raised high, then that's enough to prevent an edge from catching. If you feel yourself continually catching edges, you're not riding in the NBP; once you lock that down, however, the problem goes away.

Whether you're an experienced snowboarder or not, go ahead and rejoice: if you make turns according to my methods I've described here, you'll never catch an edge again. If you're first learning to snowboard using my no-fall technique, consider yourself lucky that I got to you first. You never, ever have to experience this fate: you can wipe the phrase "catching an edge" from your vocabulary now.

Step 6—Make Friends with the Lift

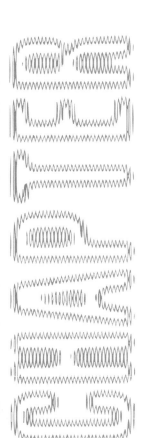

When learning how to fly, say, an airplane, one must first learn how to take off and land. After an aviation student completes enough takeoffs and landings, the nascent pilot qualifies for the next stage of instruction.

Not so in snowboarding. Safely and successfully navigating the chairlift—and all the other ways to get up the hill, from tows to T-bars—without falling is a huge issue for every rider, but especially for beginning boarders. But getting onto the mountain presents a catch-22: in order to use a chairlift, you need to know how to snowboard. But if you've never snowboarded before, you still need to get up the hill, so you have to use the chairlift.

Huh? Yes, it's a chicken-or-the-egg moment on the mountain. To help resolve this paradox, what we're going to do here in the no-fall snowboarding universe is take the element of surprise out of the chairlift experience. Everything that may trip you up on the lift, I will help you through here, mentally preparing you to anticipate and conquer any obstacle in advance.

This chapter will utterly demystify the chairlift ride for riders of any skill level. After my instruction, you'll be prepared and ready to ride the chairlift without incident.

The chairlift is a bigger issue than you might think. "Many snowboarders and skiers have a fear of heights, like when riding off the ground on a chairlift," explains Dr. Roger Callahan, co-author of *Tapping the Healer Within* and a clinical psychologist acclaimed for his work in "healing" phobias. "Fear of heights is what I encounter most—fear of getting on and off the chairlift, especially. Some patients were traumatized when the chairlift stopped when still at a high place; they were in terror. Some have a morbid feeling about getting hurt, even though they are not doing things that warrant that fear: the remote possibility they could fall and, say, get a concussion and be in a coma for the rest of their life is so small, it's not worth considering. That's a phobia—a fear that doesn't make sense, even to the person that has it."

The Chairlift Condition: Lifts, Trams, Gondolas, Tows, and T-Bars

Lifts are a big part of the sport. You will be using lifts throughout your snowboarding life, so you might as well maintain good relations with them. After all, anywhere from 4 to 10 percent of injuries that occur during snowboarding happen in the time the rider spends waiting in chairlift lines or using the lifts themselves.

As well, statistics prove that chairlifts put boarding novices at increased risk: a greater number of beginners—and those aged from ten through nineteen years old—receive injuries via lift mishaps than do more skilled, often older riders (*The American Journal of Sports Medicine*, Paul J. Abbott, January 1, 2004). Furthermore, tumbles that happen when a rider is in line for the chairlift often result in knee injury—giving the rider an even greater interest in not falling (www.aafp.org).

When you're straight-gliding off a chairlift and suddenly someone zooms in front of you, you have to make a quick decision. As well, your body must respond in kind with a trained, instinctual movement to get you outta Dodge. You simply need to avoid them as efficiently as possible—missing an obstacle by an inch is enough: you still haven't hit anything, have you?

These are the kinds of decisions I have to make every time I get on and off a chairlift. To minimize any surprises, I plan for my lift ride *before* it happens.

Troubleshooting the lift is perennially one of the most intimidating things for the novice snowboarder. The funny thing is you—yes *you*, early boarder though you may be—you already know how to safely use the chairlift. That's right: everything you need to know to get on and off the lift you've *already learned* in your very first day learning to snowboard no-fall style.

Those basics you've mastered in pages previous—skating, dragging your heel and toe to control speed, moving in a balanced straight-glide position with an unstrapped back foot—are the exact same skills that will keep you entering and exiting the chairlift in one piece. The sequence of events I describe here is applicable every time you use a lift anywhere.

Charlift Sequence 1: Getting on the Lift Successfully

A. Skate through the lift line with your front foot locked into the binding and the back foot free.

B. Try to get your own chair. If you're not experienced at riding chairlifts by yourself, the first thing you want to do is make sure you don't have anyone competing for the same chair—especially a skier or snowboarder who rides with his front foot opposite from you (see below, "The Skier Situation").

C. Wait your turn before skating up to the loading zone. When you are up, move forward to stand with the tip of your board perpendicular with the load line, your free foot supporting you in front or in back of your snowboard.

D. To position yourself to sit properly and let the lift scoop you up effortlessly, point the snowboard straight up the hill, aligning your body to stand sideways towards the oncoming chair.

E. As the chair approaches, put your hand on the back of the chair to guide yourself into your seat, sitting down on your back hip.

If you're riding the chairlift alone, always sit in the center seat so the lift doesn't tilt uncomfortably. Most chairlifts have safety bars, which I'd recommend bringing down—but first make sure anyone riding with you knows the bar is coming down. Some lifts in older resorts don't have safety bars, so you just have to hold on and hang tough. It's a little uncomfortable, but that's all you need to do. You'll be fine.

F. As the chair scoops you up, stay seated on your back hip until the snowboard leaves the ramp.

G. Once the chair is aloft, shift to a comfortable seated position, making sure both feet are pointing straight ahead and your board sits at an angle to your body.

H. If there is a footrest, use it by placing the snowboard up, over and around the rest peg. If no foot rest is provided and you need to relieve some of the weight on your front foot, try resting the back of the board on the toe of your back boot.

LIFT HAZARD 101: COPING WITH THE *"SKIER SITUATION"*

This is the point where if you are sitting next to skiers, your equipment may get tangled a bit if you're not careful. Be strategic: try to not sit next to a skier on a chairlift.

If you are unable to avoid the situation, ask your skier neighbor, "Please don't place your pole in front of my board when we exit the chairlift." The response will be a good gauge of the tenor and intensity of local skier-boarder relations.

To resolve this potentially hazardous predicament, some last, er, up-lifting words of advice: be polite to your fellow lift riders, but most importantly, whatever you do, try to make sure your lift rides are skier-free until you're more comfortable with the whole lift process. You *don't* want to have two skiers surrounding you the first time up. Tell them you're a novice—tell them anything to make *them* wait for another chair. Nicely, of course.

I don't mean to put skiers down necessarily, but they sometimes make my students nervous, often for a good reason. Riding with skiers your first time using a lift can be a little anxiety-provoking. You see, skiers slide away in straight line off the lift by planting their poles and pushing themselves off. To exit a lift, a snowboarder ideally wants to turn and sit on the back hip so that the snowboard points straight off the ramp. What inevitably happens, however, is the skier sitting next to you plants a pole in front of your snowboard and you wipe out!

I don't mean to be so hard on skiers. Really. Such problems can even come from your own kind: if you are seated next to an opposite-footed snowboarder, the tips and tails of your boards may knock together. Just being aware of these scenarios, along with making decisions on where you'll sit in the lift, and with whom, *before* you get to the chair—such approaches are your no-fall key to eliminating potentially confusing, dangerous, and ultimately unnecessary chairlift challenges.

So, after a nice ride up the chair lift it is time to get off. What are we going to do now?

Chairlift Sequence 2: Exiting the Lift with Style and Grace

Breaking news (not really): most chairlift off-ramps have been built for skiers to come off of, resulting in another adventure in chairlift land for snowboarders: steep off-ramps.

Lift off-ramps can seem intimidatingly steep at first. Often, only newer-styled ramps have the gradient to accommodate snowboard landings. Some of those old-school style lift ramps can be more like ski jumps: a dramatic incline that skiers can tilt their skis down onto and push off into from the chair. That's no fun for new riders, so that's why you want to know exactly how to get off the lift regardless of any off-ramp condition.

Fortunately, you do already: to exit the lift, you merely straight-glide off, then choose to go left or right. It's the same exact thing you practiced down on the bunny hill. If you want to go left, raise left shoulder, or vice versa. If you do this sequence while using balanced-position methods, your chairlift exit should prove smooth sailing.

Memorizing this sequence prepares the rider for a variety of scenarios we'll discuss throughout this section. In the best case, when you exit at the top of the lift there'll be no one in your way, and the ramp won't be too steep. Alas, that ideal situation isn't bloody likely most of the time. Here's what to do, in sequence, to successfully anticipate problems and exit the chairlift with ease:

A. Towards the end of the chairlift ride, watch for signs indicating it's time to raise the safety bar. You'll need to put the safety bar up to push off; as well, this is a good time to get yourself properly poised to exit when the chair hits the top.

B. To avoid group post-ramp wipeout, check with the other people on the lift as to which direction they are heading off to. Even if you're riding in a country where the locals don't speak your language, lift riders have to communicate which way everyone is going.

C. As you approach the top, turn so that you are sitting on your back hip. This position—the same one you assumed to get on the chairlift successfully—will make your board point straight ahead: it's now perfectly ready to ride in a straight-glide down and off the ramp.

D. When the snowboard comes into contact with the snow, the edge will engage, sending the snowboard in whatever direction the board's nose is pointing.

If you do not assume this position prior to getting off the chairlift, the board could end up pointing in any number of directions other than straight ahead. Exiting haphazardly like this could result in a serious leg or groin twist, or you just might meet that skier sitting next to you a few feet down in a crash.

E. Support yourself with your hands on the front edge of the chair seat for support as you prepare to exit the lift. As your snowboard comes in contact with the snow on the ramp, stand up into your straight-glide position: immediately place 51 percent of your weight on the front foot and your free back foot on the stomp-pad directly in front of the back binding. As you stand, let the chair push you into motion.

5. Going straight off the ramp in a straight-glide is your best first choice, but it isn't always an option. If someone has crashed in front of you, or if the person sitting next to you suddenly starts falling in your direction, or any other obstacle enters your path, you will need to avoid them. Just when you are getting ready and anticipating your next moves, someone ahead of you might stop directly in your path.

By straight-gliding, you are able to go any one of three ways—left, right, or straight—to avoid collision. Once you've scoped the exit area in front of you, raise your shoulder in the best direction you wish to move in and *go*.

6. As you glide down the ramp, you will slowly come to a stop. Make sure you immediately skate out of the direct ramp area, making way for the next person off the lift.

For anyone getting off a lift, getting out of the way is job one after landing safely. Nobody wants to run into someone just standing in the middle of the ramp. Once you land an airplane, you get it off the runaway. You don't want to leave it dawdling at the end of the runway when planes are landing all around every twenty seconds.

Other Ways Up the Mountain: The Gondola, T-Bar, and Tow Rope—They Don't Call 'Em "Drags" for Nothing

In addition to the most common, detachable-style chairlift, a feature of ski-resort technology since it was invented in 1936 by Jean Pomagalski for the French alpine-transport company Poma (www.pomagroup.com), there are a few other ways to get up and down the mountain that I'd recommend you get real familiar with in advance. Sometimes you just don't know what kind of lift you'll run into up there. Some runs may be serviced only by a particular kind of lift; some of the best runs, especially on glaciers and at older resorts, have the worst lift transit options.

Basically, mountain transportation breaks down into three basic food groups: chair lifts, gondolas, and the aptly named "drags"—tow ropes, T-bars and the like. It's important to know how to handle each kind. Chair lifts you know by now, but the others most likely need some introduction:

GONDOLAS

"Gondolas" are the Cadillac of the hill: per the name, they're boat-like, enclosed, elevator-type structures. On a gondola, you simply walk on and start enjoying the view. Some are sit-down affairs, typically sitting four per gondola; some are big enough that large parties crowd in and stand around like on a city bus.

As a beginning snowboarder, you mostly need to pay attention to where to store your snowboard on the gondola. Some, typically the smaller ones where passengers sit, feature a rack on the outside of the door to hold your snowboard; in the bigger variety, you typically bring the snowboard inside with you. After that, just enjoy the ride.

TOWS AND T-BARS: THE BIGGEST DRAG ABOUT SNOWBOARDING

Tows and T-Bars are both drag lifts, and most boarders I know consider them "drags" as well. Hardy-har, I know, but it's true: when drag lifts were invented many moons ago, snowboards didn't merit a speck in God's eye. Drag lifts today are typically used to ferry boarders and skiers over distances too short to merit a chairlift.

If ridden incorrectly, drag lifts can prove immensely frustrating and result in injuries, like groin pulls, that could shut down your snowboarding vacation. But don't forget, you have the tools to beat any "drag" on the mountain. Let's start with . . .

Tow Ropes

Tow ropes rule the bunny hill—a place where you might spend some quality time early in your snowboard schooling, so it's good to prepare for them. Tow ropes are just what they sound like: a rope, circulating on a motorized pully, that you grab on to so they drag you to the top of the run.

The tow rope can pull you off your feet, causing you to fall down and maybe get run over by the still-moving rider behind you. Therefore, it's best to use this lift in the most strategic manner possible. It's actually pretty easy if you put your mind to it.

1. As you step up to the toe rope, get into the balanced straight-glide position.
2. Take the rope in your hands, letting the rope run through your fingers.
3. As you close your grip, the motion of the rope will pull you along.
4. Bend your back knee, putting just a little bit more weight on your back foot as you mosey up the incline.
5. When you arrive at the exit point, let go and step off the board.

T-Bars and Their Ilk: The Hardest Button to Button

Holler if you enjoy placing a cold aluminum bar between your legs and allowing it to drag you via motor up a mountain. No, I didn't holler either! What I'm describing is not a medieval torture device, but a modern one: an all-too-common drag lift invented, naturally, by and for skiers.

T-bars and their ilk are sadistically simple: a piece of metal shaped like a "T," capable of pulling two skiers, each sitting on either side of the back bar, up an incline. A "J" bar is like a T-bar, but designed just for one skier; meanwhile, "button" lifts, which you find all over European winter resorts, are similar to T- and J-bars but with a plastic/metal "button" instead of a letter to put between the skier's legs.

Note I didn't say snowboarder—button lifts are not designed for optimum snowboard use: unlike skis, snowboards aren't designed to be pulled up hill at all. Because you're standing sideways on your board, any pulling uphill on a drag lift is going to be uncomfortable. But T-bars and their counterparts can be essayed without terror, and with as little discomfort as possible. Fun stuff, I know—I don't want to stick a button behind my butt any more than you do, but sometimes they creep up on you in the unlikeliest places. Regardless, here's how to conquer this alternative "drag."

T-Bars, J-Bars 'n Buttons . . .

1. Standing in the straight-glide position, slide up to the T-bar, J-bar or button device, keeping yourself standing sideways.

Some drag lifts are designed to pull you from behind your hip, like a T- or J-bar. Some, like a button, feature a bent aluminum tube with a button on the end. Grab the tube and it moves you uphill; for support, stick it between your legs, pulling you against the inside thigh of your front leg. I tell you, a drag lift is not a very . . . ladylike experience: some you just hold on to, like a tow rope. Yet remember, all these lift options are doable, even if they're not ideal. And if you don't believe me, just try walking uphill once . . .

2. Put your loose back foot on the board. Grab the drag-lift pole with both hands, being careful not to twist at the waist.
3. Stand sideways and either rest your back hip on the bar or place the button between your legs, depending on which "drag" you get stuck with. Allow the lift to pull you up the line. As it pulls out, stabilize yourself.

You might be able to ride two people on a T-bar, but it's just not comfortable, especially for beginners. You just want to be able to stay in your straight-glide stance and not vary from it, without unnecessary distraction.

4. When you approach the top of the drag lift, remove the support device. Keep holding on to the pole, however, allowing it to drag you until you reach the exit area.

5. Let go of the pole and skate away, *brah*.

It's time for a new set of congratulations: you've just conquered some of the finest ski technology the late nineteenth century had to offer—before it conquered you. To cope with any of the drag-lift variations you might encounter, remember the key to swinging any drag lift lies in constantly maintaining your straight-glide position. In any of them, the snowboarder basically straight-glides one-footed while being pulled uphill. Some people even like having both feet strapped in when they ride these devices. If you're scared or have any questions before you get on, speak to the lift operator.

But really, was that so bad? You have now conquered the lift, that most necessary evil of mountain riding, and it didn't prove so evil after all. To boldly go where most humans fear to tread, we sometimes need to take public transportation. Even the most super-extreme athletes have such problems. The surfers on Hawaii's North Shore that innovated big-wave riding eventually had to be towed into the biggest waves on Jet Skis because they could no longer catch them any other way. If they can do it, so can you. By the time you finish this book, I hope you already have.

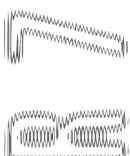

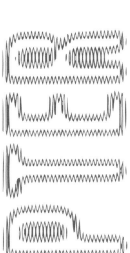

Step 7—Learn to Read Terrain

> "Can't cheat the mountain, pilgrim—
> mountain's got its own ways
>
> *—Bear Claw*

Bear Claw is a character from *Jeremiah Johnson*, probably the greatest mountain-man movie ever made. Released in 1972 but set in the 1800s, this classic features Robert Redford as the titular protagonist, a mysterious nomad not scared by "ghostly stories about the tall hills." Jeremiah shuns city-folk ways and lives off the land by his own wits, giving up civilized society for an unpredictable but soul-expanding life lived high up in the Colorado Rockies. In many ways, Jeremiah learns to become the ultimate "terrain reader" just to be able to survive.

Reading terrain is the "using the force" of snowboarding. It's both the easiest and the most difficult thing about the sport. It's easiest because it can't be divorced from the doing: you only "learn" terrain by actually snowboarding. It's the hardest because the amount of knowledge one can acquire while learning terrain is endless. I can't teach you to read any particular terrain, but I can help you prepare for it.

So far, I've encouraged you to ride in snow conditions that are ideal for the beginning rider: smooth, consistent terrain. But there's more to the mountain than that—even on those easier runs you might run into a hairy surprise—and you want to be prepared.

When Luke Skywalker had to learn "the force" in *Star Wars*, he trained his reflexes to anticipate the unknown. Don't forget—the young Jedi took a few surprise zaps before he got it right, and you will too. Like sage ol' Bear Claw said above, "the mountain's got its own ways," so you'd best prepare as much as possible.

Reading terrain relies on two senses: vision and feel. When snowboarding, you're always looking ahead and around to see what's coming, and then adjusting yourself accordingly to avoid terrain that's not optimum. If you can't avoid that terrain, you ride through it as best you can, filing away in your brain what was successful or not about that effort for future use in similar situations.

The reading-terrain process is analogous to driving a car. You're constantly scanning the road ahead, making sure you don't hit a pothole, or checking your blind spot before changing lanes. Sometimes you have no choice but to hit the pothole; in that case, you have to be in the most aggressive position possible to absorb it and steer.

Riding snow, however, it's harder to see the potholes. Mountain terrain is constantly changing; the good news is that the more you ride, the larger you store of experience from which you can draw.

Consider this: a typical ski run is made up of millions and millions—

maybe *zillions*—of individual snowflakes. If every snowflake, as the cliché goes, is different, then that makes for near-infinite amounts of terrain variation. That's not adding in other variables, like, say, weather: is the temp so cold that the snow has turned to ice? Or has spring (read slush) come early?

Then there's wear and tear to consider—a run that's been ridden many times over is going to be different from one that's never been ridden before. Time of day is also a factor; as temperatures and shadow fluctuate throughout the day, snow melts, freezes, and remelts, in an order decided on capriciously by the God of Snow Sports and no one else.

"Reading terrain," therefore, consists of the rider's ability to retain what it's like to ride a certain terrain, and to skillfully retap that memory when confronted with something similar. Other activities like mountain biking, surfing, skateboarding, and even walking can give you reading-terrain practice. Still, there ain't nothing like the real thing, baby: the more terrain you ride, the more knowledge you gain, and the better you'll snowboard. Period.

But let's not get ahead of ourselves in this quest for knowledge. A snowboarding beginner should always look for terrain that's perfectly groomed and smooth, and as consistent as possible—no surprises, just smooth sliding, very nice.

Only when you're ready to challenge yourself should you try tougher, more varied runs; always gradually and systematically build up to the more advanced stuff. In some cases, the terrain will change by the millisecond under your feet: you need to build up to that experience by taking in as much gentle, not-too-steep, groomed terrain as possible.

That said, even on the easiest of runs you'll still snowboard into a surprise or two that'll test your skills. You'll find yourself learning how to read terrain whether you like it or not. You might hit a series of bumps, or "moguls," caused by the pile-up left behind by riders and skiers. You might find yourself on top of a thinly disguised patch of ice, or slush for that matter. Even soft, dreamy "powder," the Holy Grail of snowboard terrain conditions, features its own challenges for the less experienced rider.

The great thing about reading terrain is that it is truly individual and uncompetitive. Snowboarders don't go to the *après-ski* bar and get into drunken fights about who is the best terrain reader. It's also the greatest place of growth in snowboarding's learning cycle, yet with the most slyly imperceptible progress: after thirty-plus years of snow-sports experience, my anticipatory skills are still expanding.

It doesn't take years, however, to gain confidence. "If you run over a bump, you can feel it, but you still have to get the nervous signals to acuate the muscles that are going to compensate," explains David Lind, professor emeritus of physics at the University of Colorado at Boulder and an expert in the physics of snow sports. "If you feel it, you don't have to rely on the signals from the eye to the brain as much. A slalom skier who has to move through a series of gates does so through anticipation. He has already 'programmed in' what the sequence has got to be."

What Lind describes here, my friends, is the "it" which Bruce Lee considers the key to making his martial-arts training reflexive. " It is when you act with unconscious awareness—you just act," Lee once said. "Like when you throw a ball to me and, without thought, my hands go up and catch it." The movements I'm showing you in no-fall snowboarding are the exact moves you want to make instinctual; they are the ones that allow you to access fully the "it" of reading terrain.

If you practice those moves and learn them, the next time you're out on the hill bombing around and you feel yourself go out of balance, you'll know exactly how to move and reclaim that balance to save yourself from falling. That's the "it" working. In order to get to that point, you have to do a lot of work, absorbing the moves you want to dial in.

Reading terrain really is the fusion of Zen and the art of no-fall snowboarding: it's going to happen anyway—you'll find yourself reading terrain whether you intend to or not, determining where you want to go and how you're going to get there. When it comes to riding different, sometimes challenging, terrain, I'm a cup-is-half-full guy. I like to snowboard in all conditions: I find most every terrain has some thrilling, fun-to-ride aspect, even if it holds challenges that are scary at first.

Besides, you do not want to be that person who balks because a run is too bumpy, or steep, or whatever. Sometimes you may not have a choice in the matter. In snowboarding as in life, you're going to face "terrain" that's intimidating, but you still have to get down past it. You might as well have all the tools handy to figure out the best way down, and enjoy it, too.

The following are my tried-and-true no-fall methods to making friends with any terrain you might come across on the mountain. You'll discover in your terrain-reading adventures that the snowboard technique you've already learned from this book is your best safety net—you just need to adapt the aggressiveness of your riding to what's happening in the moment, on the hill, all the time.

Flats and Straights

Polls have shown snowboarders dread the "flats"—the areas on a ski mountain where there's very little incline—more than they do physical injury! But while encountering flats is inevitable, they aren't that bad, really, so you might as well triumph over them.

Skiers have poles to push them through the flats; snowboarders, alas, don't. Therefore, the first rule of conquering the horizontal plane is *anticipation.* You want to anticipate the flats coming up, then increase and maintain as much speed as possible to ride through them without stopping until you reach a steeper area. As you ride down runs, try to perceive in advance how they might peak and valley. See if you can anticipate a rhythm to the pitch that will carry you through to the next run.

When you become comfortable with riding your edges, or "carving," then you won't have to worry about maintaining momentum over flatter terrain. By really riding your edge in these conditions, you're creating less momentum-killing friction skid, allowing you to hold your speed better. To optimally ride a snowboard on flat terrain, absorb the following coping approaches.

STRAIGHT SHOOTING THE FLATS

If you encounter flat terrain on the mountain, like a long horizontal stretch peppered with obstacles or a catwalk (a narrow trail connecting ski runs), you need more than anything to travel in a straight line here.

1. To achieve this, stand steady in the NBP. Put 51 percent of your weight on the front foot, which will engage the maximum available gravity, causing you to straight-glide on through. As long as you keep your weight off the back foot and don't twist the body around, you should continue straight-gliding down the fall line regardless of your desired speed.

   Be careful to maintain balance while straight-gliding flats. Dropping out of the NBP will cause your snowboard to skid, opening up your downhill edge to "catch an edge"; that'll send you tumbling like a rug got pulled out from under you.

2. If you feel your momentum decreasing, try bending the knees and lowering through their full range of motion. The more quickly and aggressively you execute this movement, the more noticeably your velocity will increase.

3. If there are variations in the snow, which there always are, you can adjust with minute turns. Steer back and forth with slight shoulder movements to keep yourself locked in the fall-line at almost any speed.

4. To carve in the *heel-side* direction to, say, avoid an obstacle, then raise your front shoulder while simultaneously lowering the back shoulder, as always.

5. To make a more aggressive, abrupt turn, combine an even greater shoulder movement with a commensurate adjusting bend of the knees and ankles.

6. Ride this arc across the catwalk until you wish to initiate a *toe-side* turn, in which you repeat the above process as necessary with your back shoulder. You'll be out of slow-moving traffic in no time.

If you want to have fun riding flats, carrying speed is key—in fact, taking the mountain's more horizontal areas at slower speeds is actually harder. An ice-skating rink is flat, yet people who ice skate have no problem getting around at various speeds. The secret to maintaining speed on flats is getting on your edge and carving like you're at the ice rink. Soon you'll be making elegant carves on flats with intensity.

Bumps 'n Troughs

When snowboarding, you may come upon a field of "moguls"—sizable bumps created by skiers carving through loose, ungroomed terrain. Many advanced skiers *love* to zip through moguls.

Snowboarders, however, often find getting through bumps a grind. But that's because most people are taught to snowboard as if they're skiing on one ski. Skiers are taught to attack the fall-line, making turns back and forth across it as quickly and symmetrically as possible. That works fine for a skier, and a snowboard can simulate the same line as skier, but why? Skis and snowboards aren't the same equipment, so they shouldn't be ridden as if they are.

Furthermore, a mogul field is an extreme environment, so you have to be equally extreme in your movements to compensate. If you're not 100 percent on the ball riding bumps, the odds of you falling are high. When I hit bumps, I make one turn at a time, taking each turn very aggressively, carrying speed over a steep and inconsistent terrain. What makes doing moguls fun is they make me use all my physical ability to propel myself down the mountain in control.

People complain about moguls because it's aggressive terrain; upon discovering an unexpected bumps field on a run, many think "Oh great, I'm gonna be exhausted after this—my day on the hill is done." If you're not working with the snowboard, it's working against your body: you're absorbing immense torques and pressure against your legs that causes uncomfortable physical strain.

In other words, if you don't like rollercoasters, don't ride them.

In a mogul field, you'll come across two specific kinds of terrain: bumps (piles of snow built up throughout the run) and troughs (the channel carved out between each bulge in the snow). If you can conquer these two types of terrain and the turns necessary to ride them, you're in for a smooth, fun, but above all *exhilarating* run.

With bumps and troughs, the rider wants to make best use of the shape of the snowboard. The curve of the snowboard complements the shape of the bump, almost like it's a missing piece of a puzzle, allowing the rider to follow it around.

NAVIGATING BUMPS

1. To begin, start with the downhill edge of your snowboard on the uphill side of any bump you might encounter.
2. Allow the snowboard to move *around* the middle of the bump until you reach the bump's downhill side.
3. Once there, ride across the trough separating this bump from the next, at which point you'll raise your shoulder and switch to ride the opposite edge, putting you into position to ride the next bump you encounter in the same way.

GETTING THROUGH TROUGHS

1. Look for troughs hollowed out into a concave shape that has a nice bank on it. Your snowboard can best follow this shape, giving you a good platform to control speed and direction. At the end of these troughs, there will inevitably be another bump.

2. Ride through the trough into the middle of the next bump's uphill angle. Switch your shoulders to initiate the opposite edge and you'll be in the perfect position to ride around this bump. Lay the edge right in the middle of the next bump, and you're now ready to ride around it.

3. Ride the remaining series of bumps and troughs by alternating your shoulder steer. Take them one at a time, all the while maintaining balance at a slow and controlled pace. Hold back from going faster until riding this surface environment in such a manner feels natural.

Because you are in advanced and challenging terrain, you'll need to be able to ride as aggressively as the terrain dictates. Be ready to use your full range of motion in your shoulders and lower body to maintain balance.

Connecting bumps and troughs in this manner is a great way to ride through this terrain.

Just knowing these two things to look for—bumps and troughs—will arm you with enough terrain-reading ability to make your way down the most challenging ungroomed slopes. You'll most likely find bumps now both stimulating and demanding at the same time. I find when I'm riding bumps with maximum performance it's a *blast:* my board flows and turns like I'm on the ultimate natural roller coaster.

Ice and Icy Conditions: Don't Tread On Me

Ice takes away all the brakes: riding a snowboard on its slick surface, you really start hauling *ass.* In any snow sport, the highest speeds are most attainable riding ice; sometimes I just like to take it for all it's worth and bomb down that frozen surface all the way to the bottom at maximum velocity.

Ice is fast, and it's difficult to quickly change direction on it if you are skidding. To that end, one must start carving aggressively, pushing the shoulders and knees through their full range of motion to engage the snowboard's razor-sharp edge to make it *turn.*

Whether you're on an icy patch at the bottom of the bunny hill or dropped off-piste via helicopter in the middle of a chunky Arctic glacier, try to choose a path that allows the snowboard to complete a full turn through the ice. This means that you'll be held stable as your board's finely honed steel edge grips the unforgivingly slick ice. This is where reading the terrain comes into play: once you acknowledge you're on ice, choose the shape of the turning arc you wish to ride and take it as aggressively as necessary.

Corduroy:
No, Not Like Your Jeans . . .

Grooming makes the terrain consistent. "Corduroy"—machine-groomed, vertical grooves of snow that resembles its soft namesake fabric in the linear uniformity of its ribbed parallel lines—remains the preferred terrain for beginners because it's the most consistent. "Groomers" make for especially ideal terrain to explore your capacity for speed: you can use all your power to get down the hill without worrying too much about the surface condition of the snow.

That said, corduroy has its challenges. If you're not snowboarding correctly, it's easy to get an edge caught in its grooves. And while the surface should be consistent overall, the hill itself will still present little knolls and high spots as you're going down. Don't be afraid of these nuances—they can help you.

In order to keep my speed going on groomed runs, I utilize the different pitches on the hill, riding my board to the top of the run's higher spots, then putting myself back down the fall line. Even on the flattest terrain, you can pick out the high spots and then use the momentum coming off them to increase your speed. Use the subtle undulations in groomed terrain to generate momentum when needed.

What I like is springtime snowboarding, when the runs are groomed in the evening into perfect corduroy. By morning, however it's frozen-solid—bulletproof grooming. I like the way riding over the hard corduroy's surface tingles my feet, and I quickly get absorbed by the speed I can get going on it, too. Fun stuff.

Powder: Snowboard Nirvana

Powder is the snowboarder's idea of heaven: fresh, untracked snow in its natural state. Powder can come in different flavors, from the airy, light variety of Colorado and Utah to the heavier, wetter version you find in the Pacific Northwest to Montana's legendary snow so dry they call it "cold smoke."

When you're riding powder successfully, it literally feels like you're floating in space; it's pillow soft, too. Powder can also be forgiving, and not just on impact. Sometimes, if you make a mistake, the give of the powder makes it easier to correct mid-ride while floating; this anti-gravity quality feels as if you're caught in *The Matrix*.

The key to riding "pow" no-fall style is to keep your speed up so that the board is floating. The minimum velocity necessary to keep a snowboarder floating in powder is relatively small.

However, once you find that speed, you must maintain it (or go faster); otherwise, you might get stuck. When reading powder terrain, keep one thing in mind: If you go too slow in powder, the board will start to sink in the snow! Imagine standing chest-high in snow with a snowboard strapped to your feet and your friends zipping past, having the ride of their lives.

This is not fun. You do not want to stop in powder at all unless you have enough of an incline to get started again; basically, stop at the highest possible area of the terrain you can. Even if you have to dig yourself out of chest-deep snow, though, I'll bet you find your initial powder experience revelatory. I know I did, and still do.

Going Off-Piste: Backcountry Riding Between the Lines

The "backcountry" and "off-piste" are the roads less traveled when snowboarding—hopefully not traveled at all, leaving you with untracked natural powder runs. Backcountry is snowboarding's *tabula rasa*, untainted by human "progress." These are ungroomed, and in many cases unpatrolled, ski areas. Backcountry is the apex of extreme.

As a result, backcountry can be deliberately difficult, and sometimes expensive, to get to—and potentially more dangerous. The backcountry embodies the wild outdoors, and won't let you forget it. There's no guarantee that the conditions will be ideal. It may be too steep, or not steep enough; there may not be enough snow, or there may be too much. It's up to nature, intense preparation, and a whole lotta terrain reading to get the snowboarder through.

That's why avalanches are a potential hazard in the backcountry. Regardless of your skill level, when riding this terrain make sure you have a proper guide certified in avalanche safety.

Steeps: The Final Frontier?

Steep, expert runs are the bane of many a beginning snowboarder, and there's a reason: only a daredevil isn't scared at first of the sheer, often icy and ungroomed drops of a serious black-diamond expert run.

However, your no-fall technique movements will give you all the support you need on steeps. All the increased pitch of the steeps means is that the boarder needs to ride more aggressively. You will need to read the terrain and adjust accordingly, as you will most likely be exerting your body's range of motion through its fullest extent.

Because of the extreme conditions that you are putting yourself into on steeps, you will need to be ready to move from one position to the next quickly and accurately. It's important to stay in balance and control so as not to miss a single turn.

Reading the terrain accurately on steeps allows you to make the exact, calculated moves to best achieve any tasks at hand. Really, getting yourself down off the steep face you are on safely, and having fun doing it, is the best reward.

What I like best about steeps is, you never have to worry about getting stuck—the momentum will pull you along. You have the ability to reach your desired speed most quickly on a serious incline. Your options of where to go on steep terrain are greater—you can vary your course more than on flat ground. If you have two feet of powder snow, you're going to want to be on steep terrain to really get through it. At some point soon in your snowboarding development, steeps will move permanently from the "scary" to the "fun" category.

Despite the natural thrills 'n chills of riding more extreme stuff like steeps and powder, reading terrain isn't just about taking what cards nature deals you. These days, winter resorts feature all kinds of man-made terrain, from half-pipes to terrain parks filled with jumps and jib rails.

I like to ride it *all*, personally, although I'm really mostly what's considered a "freerider." "Freeriders" are most concerned with riding as much of the mountain that they can; "freestylers," meanwhile, mostly perform tricks in man-made environments like terrain parks and half-pipes. "Slope-style" is the crossover between both factions: this kind of rider takes his freestyle repertoire of tricks to the hill, using naturally occurring variations in the terrain as his stunting launch pad.

I don't mind being called a freerider—I perceive that label to mean that I'm "free" to go anywhere I want on the mountain. Anyway, I'd rather destroy epic powder fields than huck around a big man-made ditch dug by a tractor-like "pipe dragon." To me, a terrain park is cool, but it's also kind of like swimming in a wave pool when you've got the ocean right next to you.

I'm not putting down any kind of freestyle riding at all—I understand that anything and everything you can make that snowboard do to test the limits of physical science has its own set of thrills. I love that, in snowboarding, there's room for everyone's taste. Snowboarding is so cool and democratic that, if you want to build a jump in your backyard at your parent's house in Wisconsin and huck mad tricks, you can, and most importantly, have the time of your life doing it. Or I can take a helicopter and ride natural half-pipes in the wild Alaska backcountry.

In fact, the more you choose to vary the terrain in your riding, the greater your ability to handle adverse, difficult, and changing conditions. The more you challenge yourself, the better your knowledge of useful terrain experience will become. And the more you ride different terrain, the more your body will become accustomed to the feel of new experiences—new experiences that once seemed unnatural but now have transformed into instinct.

Whatever poison you prefer terrain-wise, I just want everyone to be able to read their runs correctly so they can discover what and where they want to ride themselves. The obstacles are not just in your path, but in your mind; indeed, I think you'll be surprised how quickly and easily you leap them with practice. And even if you're doing jumps off kickers in the backyard, my technique can help you have more fun, too.

Regardless of my teachings, you'll find out for yourself that the great thing about mastering terrain to the best of your abilities is that it is a truly individual process. With that knowledge, you can now best choose where you want to go and what you will be riding on. In other words, the ability to read terrain is commensurate with your capacity for freedom.

Where You'll Find Me

"The Rocky Mountains is the marrow of the world. I ain't never seen them, but my common sense tells me the Andes is foothills and the Alps is for children to climb."

—Del Gue, *Jeremiah Johnson*

"Mont-Blanc and the Valley of Chamonix, and the Sea of Ice, and all the wonders of the most wonderful place are above and beyond one's wildest expectation. I cannot imagine anything in nature more stupendous or sublime."

—*Charles Dickens*

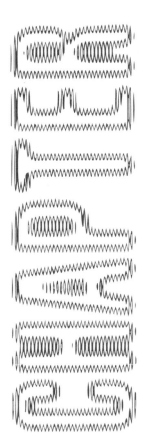

t's 2:30 in the afternoon; we've been out snowboarding since the early morning. It's late in the season, but me and Jenny are riding maybe some ten thousand feet up into the bluebird sky overlooking a massive valley in

Valgrisenche, Italy. That morning's blizzard left maybe six inches of fresh snow—we're talking wide open powder fields, rendered in different shapes and sizes by nature's whim.

The scenery is awe inspiring—an encounter with the sublime. Serrated mountain peaks of black rock surround us in all directions; glaciers spill out amidst huge cliffs, melting and shiny in the April sun. In fact, the only sound we hear is chunks of the glacier periodically dislodging off mountain walls with loud, stunning crashes. It's a steep, steep run, yet covered by many feet of the softest, pillowy snow; the intense incline actually gives us great speed, which helps cut through all that pow. Even if you were falling—which, naturally, we're not—the worst that would happen is we'd get stuck in a snow cloud.

Me and Jenny are really, really alone here on this wild, yet forgiving, untracked terrain. No other boarders or skiers cross our path anywhere in this surreal environment that resembles nothing so much as a lunar landscape.

To get to this magic place, we had to "heli-board"—that is, hire a helicopter to fly us to remote "off-piste" areas far from the groomed runs of the resort. This is real backcountry, where the best snow and vistas hide away from the crowds stuck back in civilization. Preparation to ride in such extreme environments is essential. Due to its isolated location and potential dangers, we were sure to take along a local high-mountain guide, one utterly versed in first-aid and avalanche safety.

This day proved a riding adventure bar none. Everything started around 9 a.m.—that's when we got picked up by the helicopter just down the street from our hotel, Albergo Perret, a charmingly rustic, woodsy Italian twist on the classic mountain-chalet inn. It was very rustic, in fact: the chef would cook us wild *chamois*—local mountain goat—for dinner, among other local mountain delicacies that the area's denizens have been eating for centuries. Every course served, of course, was accompanied by superb regional selections from the hotel's amazing wine-cellar "cave."

Anyways, back to heli-boarding. The swarthy guy filling the tank of our waiting chopper was smoking cigarettes very close to the fueling station as he pumped the gas. He was doing it so casually that it looked like he knew what he was doing, but I still took a few steps back. They live by different codes up here in the Alps, so I wasn't going to question it too much, though. These guys know the mountain better than anyone.

By the end of the day, Jenny and I had already shared the snowboarding journey of my dreams—of anyone's. We had gone up five or six times already, but we still wanted more.

We were addicted because, no matter where we rode, we barely encountered any adverse conditions. In the backcountry, you can come across anything, but on this day conditions were perfect, an alternately exhilarating and meditational blend of steep terrain and moderate pitch. Because the runs were so big and wide, and the fresh powder was so soft, everything was working in our favor.

Best of all, the run we chose was shaped like a gargantuan, natural half-pipe, its high, curving side-walls arching a hundred feet into the thin air. Massive distance separated its two walls—hundreds of yards spanned one side to the other. It was just *bliss*. And in this extraordinary setting, Jenny, my friend and student, made a breakthrough in her snowboarding.

Jenny had started the day a little spooked, however. The expanse, the wide openness of the terrain, and the height, not to mention having so many choices about where to go, made her irrationally unsure of what she was doing. Inside, she questioned every inch she covered, not trusting her instincts about whether the upcoming terrain was safe to ride. Understandably, someone who's not accustomed to that kind of environment might find it daunting. We were specks, infinitesimal particles waiting to be swallowed up by the mountain.

Finally, we reached the valley floor, at the end of what I thought was our last run. On this last run, everything came together perfectly for Jenny, as if by kismet. Her riding became more aggressive and lyrical at the same time; more than anything, it was confident—if Jenny saw terrain she wanted to explore, if she desired to challenge herself in her riding, she did. When Jenny turned around and looked at the curving, magnificent line she'd just rode through this imposing natural creation of rock, snow and ice, she smiled and said "Let's do that again."

Hearing those words from Jenny made me smile. Watching her ride on the last run, I saw how everything clicked for her. To be able to see that huge expanse, and then to be able to ride it—it all combined to inspire her to go anywhere and anyway she chose.

Previously, what Jenny had been most afraid of was the great white abyss. When confronted with such an all-encompassing vista, she'd get afraid she'd fall off a cliff or into a crevasse; the unknown that lay ahead freaked her out. Her issue, ultimately, was about reading the terrain—being able to see where you want to go and going there.

Jenny's terrain reading, however, clicked when she went into action. This time, she was flying along at speed: using the mountain to her advantage, she watched for peaks and valleys, adjusting accordingly to maintain momentum. What she was doing was reading terrain at the ultimate level: she was in a situation completely out of her element, yet she rose to the occasion and let her trained instincts guide her. This was not an easy "piste" run: just committing herself to getting down gave her enlightenment.

On that run, she reached the point in her snowboarding where she *understood*. She understood completely how the board worked and was able to ride the changing terrain of the mountain. Once she started riding with confidence, the trail of her carves began resembling fine calligraphy.

People dream of doing runs like this; it's everything you can imagine being just right. Location. Conditions. Situation. Time of day. They all came together at this one particular point in her riding career. At that moment, Jenny had been snowboarding for nine years. But in this extreme situation, surrounded by extreme beauty, she approached perfection. After that run, it just came upon her. Before that day in Valgrisenche, Jenny was a merely great snowboarder; afterwards, her skills became *incredible*. But there's always more to learn, which is what even the most advance boarder knows. That day, Jenny transformed her riding, and her self.

In other words, it was just another typical day at work for Danny Martin.

Okay, it wasn't typical—it was one of the really, really good days where I was able to share with my student what I most dig about snowboarding down the hill. You see, snowboarding is the best prism to see the world through. I've gone to places, seen things I never believed I would ever experience—I've seen things I never knew *existed* before I witnessed them with my own eyes.

My snowboard has become my passport to experience other cultures and bond with them, to hear different languages, sometimes three or four or ten in a day, to eat whatever cuisine is available wherever there might be snow.

I've found that almost every snowboarding trip can be exotic, however, whether it's in highest Africa or flattest Wisconsin; I've ridden everything in between, so I know. Often unexpected snowboarding destinations pleasantly surprise. I loved riding in Santa Fe in New Mexico, for example: I wasn't prepared for how nice the snow conditions would be and how steep the runs were. I liked Santa Fe's artistic bent and great food, and how the tree-lined runs have a unique, closed-in feel.

Then there are those places I haven't snowboarded yet. Asia is high up on the list; I can't wait to tackle the Himalayas, and the Japanese Alps are supposed to be incredible. I'm scheduled to go to Lebanon this year too, hiking and riding around Mount Lebanon itself. The reason I'm going to ride Lebanese slopes is that one of my clients grew up and learned to ski there as a child; to return as an adult and snowboarder there will be the culmination of a personal pilgrimage for him.

That will be the latest of many adventures I've taken around the world on the snowboard express. Someday, someway I'll probably find a way to ride on dry land. It wouldn't surprise me after all I've seen from the perspective of riding. Regardless, this chapter takes you through the many journeys I've taken around the globe in the name of snowboarding. This is not a comprehensive list of the "best" places to snowboard—although many of them are. It's merely a subjective rummaging through everywhere I've ever been in the world on a board.

I want you to be excited about the possibilities that snowboarding offers—the way it can broaden mind, body, and soul as catalyst for adventures you never thought possible. On a snowboard, you can learn a place just like you can learn a language; I can't wait for you to begin your own adventures. That's when you'll not only learn how to snowboard, but you'll fully experience all its manifold joys in the setting the sport was meant for.

Snowboarding in North America

THE POWDER DAZE OF THE EPIC WEST

Seeing the Western United States through the lens of a snowboard is one of the great joys of my life. You can travel back in time to the days of the pioneers and begin to comprehend what life must've been like in earlier times—what a struggle it must've been to conquer the West's vast, seemingly unforgiving landscape. People come from all over the world to ride America's West due to its superior conditions, incredibly varied terrain, and jaw-dropping natural beauty.

COLORADO: ROCKY MOUNTAIN HIGH

Colorado is the place I call home, so you can imagine how amazing it is. I made it my home figuring this was the best place for a snowboarder to work out of: it's centrally located, and there are plenty of famed ski areas in all directions.

As well, many ski resorts in Colorado were among the first to be snowboarding-sympathetic; as a result, a lot of snowboarding history has been made in the Colorado Rockies. Snowboard companies Never Summer and Unity were founded here; pro riders like Megan Pischke, Chad Otterstrom, Todd Richards, and the late, great Josh Malay all have represented Colorado as their home base.

And the grandeur of the Colorado Rockies remains undeniable—they *are* the marrow of the world. Covered in pine and aspen, full of wildlife everywhere, these peaks are best on the perfect bluebird days typical of a "colorful Colorado" winter.

Colorado resorts are superb for the most part, even smaller ones. Famous names always on boarders' lips include the remote Crested Butte, Steamboat Springs, Keystone, and the locals' favorite, Arapahoe Basin. Called "A-Basin" by those in the know, this pow magnet has the highest rideable area accessible by lifts in North America, its summit elevation reaching over 13,000 feet. Even better, A-Basin is often the last resort to close for the season, featuring rideable terrain until even Independence Day sometimes.

Colorado has something for every interest, all within reasonable distances of each other. Each resort offers unique variations on high-altitude snowboarding at its best—think 14,000 foot peaks, if you can. In general, I *really* like the "pow" in Colorado, where the altitude keeps snow very light and fluffy. Few experiences rival, say, "catboarding" to Vail Pass to ride waist deep in powder ("catboarding" is where, instead of a helicopter, you take a "snowcat"—a snow-invincible mini-bus—into backcountry to get fresh powder. It's glorious). Eat, sleep, snowboard—that's pretty much the foundation of every day here in the Rockies.

Aspen

The Gstaad of Colorado, Aspen is the state's snow-sports playground of the elite. How elite? Well, Aspen cops drove Saabs for twenty-five years until they switched recently, with much public outcry, to Ford Explorers. Aspen's natural resources, however, outshine any snobbery—in fact, their seeming infinity dazzles to no end. The namesake aspen trees also provide many stellar opportunities for glade riding you can't just get anywhere.

Vail

Colorado's other luxe ski area. In Vail, the powder's so nice they call it "champagne." Alas, that means champagne prices (and sometimes attitude) as well. What I like about Vail is its size: it's *huge*. You can snowboard all day without having to take the same lift.

Beaver Creek

My favorite mountain remains my local hill. Beaver Creek represents everything I like about Colorado snowboarding. I love riding glades at "The Beav": I taught at Beaver Creek for seven years, so I know the mountain better than any I've ever ridden. In fact, I consider the top of Beaver Creek my office. As well, the resort is ergonomically designed to perfection, truly evoking the feel of a classic Alpine village. Sometimes you'll even hear a guy named Helmut yodel and play the alpenhorn.

MONTANA: HIGH TIMES, INDEED

I've lived in Montana for five years, off and on, since 1986. More than anything, I feel free in Montana. As you move further north in the Rocky Mountains, they get wilder, and Montana is pretty freakin' wild. You've probably seen its landscapes in movies like *A River Runs Through It*.

Big Sky

Positioned near *über*-scenic Yellowstone Park, this remote Western resort lies smack dab in true cowboy country, with wide-open spaces big enough for cattle rustling. Everything's on a bigger scale than normal: it's no surprise this is the steepest resort in the United States. It's also legal to drive here with open liquor bottles—heck, they'll give you a to-go cup at the bar if you want (you'll need that alcohol to keep warm in often arctic temps). Montana remains most legendary for its exquisite brand of powder snow called "cold smoke"; I've never ridden anything better. Here, snowflakes the size of silver dollars fall so lightly, they stack on top of each other, blowing away like fog as you pass through it.

WYOMING: THE WHOLE OF THE WORLD

Wyoming is steep—not as vertical as Big Sky, perhaps, but absolutely picturesque and beautiful in an Old West style that one doesn't find enough in this post-millennium moment. Wyoming makes me think of the mountain-man days.

Jackson Hole

During pioneer times, Wyoming's most famous resort town was a favorite destination for fur trappers, who'd come down from the mountains to sell their pelts and restock provisions. Every time I enter Jackson, I wonder anew about what those mountain men must've thought when they first encountered its rustic beauty.

CALIFORNIA LOVE

Golden State resorts like Tahoe and Mammoth are famous, but you'll find *hella* riders at snowboarding-geared local resorts like Big Bear in the monolithic Sierra Mountain range.

Big Bear

At three thousand feet, Big Bear isn't the biggest snowgun in the West. However, Bear was one of the first resorts to incorporate special snowboard-friendly features like half-pipes and terrain parks. Bear locals—many of whom have become pro riders—rave about the sprawling backcountry. And when conditions are good, there's no denying Bear's famous "Sierra cement," a slushy, soft snow that many riders travel far and wide to tear up.

UTAH: SNOWBOARD COUNTY U.S.A.

When you get off the plane in Utah's Salt Lake City airport and look around, you're stunned: the mountain ranges that line the horizon are such perfect specimens, they're the quintessence of "mountain." Utah license plates proclaim "The Greatest Snow On Earth," which isn't too far off: resorts here often achieve record snow dumps.

Park City

A refined family resort, Park City gets a little added glamour from the proximity of Robert Redford's Sundance Film Festival. Always undeniably state of the art, Park City reinforced its connection to snowboarding with the 2002 Winter Olympics, putting in one of the world's greatest, most complete terrain parks for snowboarding events, which they continue to maintain and improve for resort visitors.

The Canyons

My favorite Utah resort. The Canyons is newish and *very* snowboard friendly—one of the few resorts that feels truly engineered for maximum snowboarding potential. Each run is groomed perfectly, designed to keep a snowboarder off flats; as well, there's a healthy terrain park 'n pipe for the jibber-centric, at enjoyably high elevation.

The Pacific Northwest:
Soul Rider Central

"Today the rain is going on strong, but . . . tomorrow, maybe the sun will come out again," Bruce Lee once said. "It's like, that type of a thing." The moody, inclement weather of the Pacific Northwest is indeed that type of thing—and Bruce Lee should know: after his death in 1973, Lee was laid to rest in Lake View Cemetery in his beloved Seattle, Washington.

But all that rain means a whole lotta snow in the winter. Not surprisingly, some of the most legendary North American snowboarding areas are in the Pacific Northwest, which remains the apex for "soul riding."

I resist such categories, but if I had to slot myself into a box I'd probably consider myself a "soul rider" over all else. The term refers to a freeriding snowboarder who above all wishes to preserve his or her integrity—who rides for him- or herself as an individual above all else.

Instead of competing in races, "soul riders" compete against themselves only. Like a combination of new-school mountain man à la *Jeremiah Johnson* and defiant Fugazi-style punk rocker, the "soul rider" often forgoes mainstream society for a life devoted to contemplating the mountain via snowboard.

"Soul riders" aspire to spiritual inspiration by going back to the roots of the sport, riding as much of the mountain as they can. It's spiritual side of big-time snowboarding. The most famous "soul rider" in snowboarding history is Craig Kelly, and it's no surprise that he called the Pacific Northwest home before his 2003 death in a freak avalanche accident.

Kelly gave up pro sponsorship and fame to ride for himself, studying to become a backcountry guide so he could spend as much time as possible riding and absorbing the uniqueness of British Columbia's Rocky Mountains he loved. No doubt, much of the inspiration for "soul riders" like Kelly stems from the magical Pacific Northwest terrain itself, which often conjoins sea and snow for vistas that are startling in their primordial majesty, like the landscapes in the *Lord of the Rings* movies. (*Lord of the Rings* was actually shot in New Zealand, which is said to have some of the most beautiful natural riding terrain around, too. I *can't wait* to snowboard in New Zealand!)

The Pacific Northwest's proximity to the ocean does impart a variability to the region's conditions: you might have to sit out a day or two due to fog, and the snow can be wetter and heavier than other powder varieties. The positive side of such Pacific meteorological conditions, though, is that the season often lasts much longer than other places, with some of the greatest snowfall amounts in all of North America. Many Northwest resorts stay open deep into summer, some all year round.

ALASKA: ARCTIC BEAUTY

Alyeska:

Alaska's most well-known resort. Alaska is truly God's country, and it's a privilege to ride it. I was continually staggered by the sight of sparkling glaciers erupting out of bays as I rode its runs. Before our government leaders pass yet another bill allowing our ecosystem to be further destroyed, I'd love to take them snowboarding around Alaska first. Maybe then they'd realize that stuff is worth keeping around after all.

OREGON: RIDE ALL YEAR ROUND!

Mt. Hood

One of the most unique snowboarding experiences one can enjoy is at Mt. Hood, Oregon's famed resort: it's open year round except for a couple weeks after Labor Day. That makes the atmosphere truly exciting—there are always pro athletes training or teaching nearby, and facilities are kept up to caliber. While located in a national forest, Hood's runs lie above the tree line, causing its bare, pointy peaks to resemble an otherworldly sci-fi landscape. It's so eerily cinematic, iconoclastic genius filmmaker Stanley Kubrick chose to shoot exteriors for his classic supernatural thriller *The Shining* at Hood's fantastic Timberline Lodge. But what impressed me most about Mount Hood was the respect riders there have for the sport—and each other—self-policing pipes and runs with integrity.

WESTERN CANADA: THE BEAUTY OF BRITISH COLUMBIA.

In many ways, British Columbia remains the land that time forgot—but that doesn't mean it isn't sophisticated. The Canadian Rockies comprise some of the most epic terrain ever; by the time the Rockies get up to Canada, you're in and amongst glaciers and remote wilderness. Cat and heli-boarding make up a big part of the BC experience, too, as do finer accommodations and restaurants.

Fernie's Island Lake Lodge

Fernie is one of my favorite snowboarding adventures. This resort offers an amazingly wide expanse of terrain, making for one of my favorite adventure spots. The surrounding area looks like the moon; it's definitely out of this world to ride. To get there, you have to ride a snowcat for an hour or so up the mountain, depositing you at an isolated, private lodge up at the top. There first-class dining, massages, and saunas await—everything you need to unwind after a full day of hardcore snowboarding. During one Fernie trip, the powder was so deep, I would ride through walls of snow that ended up covering my whole body.

Whistler-Blackcomb

Many consider Whistler-Blackcomb to be the greatest snow-sport institution around. According to boardtheworld.com, in 1996 alone each of the three most important ski magazines rated it at the very top. It's also as cosmopolitan as ski areas get, all while providing two amazing mountains holding over 5,000 feet of vertical and more than *ten square miles* of rideable, varied terrain. The drinking water is delicious in Whistler; it's like bottled mineral water on tap. Whistler also has one of the longest seasons in North America, and the snow often stays good until very late. You might even get a "pow day" in June.

East Coast Riding: Ice, Ice Baby

While hardly as expansive, steep, or tall as their Western counterparts—and often a hell of a lot colder—the mountain ranges lining the eastern

United States remain hotbeds of snowboard activity. Combining granola crunchiness—Ben & Jerry's, Phish, and Burton Snowboards were all spawned here—along with quaint New England vibes, the East can be a most appealing place to ride. Meanwhile, unforgiving conditions have bred riders of ingenuity and skill that can ride anything: top snowboard pro and Olympic silver medalist Danny Kass earned his stripes riding in New Jersey, for example, before going on to be an international star.

VERMONT: SNOWBOARDING'S HERITAGE

Stratton

Arguably the birthplace of modern snowboarding: Jake Burton founded the now-monolithic Burton Snowboard company here. As a result, Stratton remains a snowboarding hotspot—legendary snowboarding Olympic gold-medalist Ross Powers is a Stratton local. Terrain here isn't steep compared to, say, Colorado, and the weather can get glacially cold, which results in lotsa ice, ice, baby. Still, Stratton's well-tended park and half-pipe—which often host major snowboard contests—make for freestyler heaven.

Killington

Probably the biggest resort in Vermont, with nearly two square miles of runs and dozens of lifts. They need them. Its proximity to major cities like Boston and New York means Killington's crowds can be overpowering.

Jay Peak

My favorite place to board on the East Coast. Close enough to the Canadian border to accept Canuck cash at face value, Jay Peak's pretty remote.

Like other New England resorts it gets darn cold. However, Jay Peak comes about as close as you're going to get to true big-mountain riding outside the West. That's because, with annual snowfall ranging from three to four hundred inches, Jay gets almost as much white stuff as some of its Western counterparts—and more than any other Eastern winter-sport area. A Jay "pow day" is as awesome as anywhere, and the glade riding is righteous. If you're in the neighborhood, you can't do any better than riding at Jay.

The Midwest: Heartland Hucking in the Tall Grass

The Midwest often gets slammed as an un-ideal snowboarding destination, and I might not ever travel there just to snowboard. But Skyline Skiway in Devils Lake, North Dakota is where I first learned to ski. I'd make my way down short, sheer-ice runs on antique army-surplus planks with leather boots that locked into bindings that didn't even release.

When I was a kid, Skyline was my winter wonderland. There were two tow ropes and three runs, one of which was called "Suicide," with a vertical drop of just over three hundred feet. If you wanted to get powder, you had to wander into the tall grass, because that's where the wind would blow it away. The thought of it still makes me happy. It brings back good memories every time I go back—I go by and pay my respects each time I visit my family.

Being from the Midwest, I know how flat the middle of the U.S.A. can be, and yes, the frigid cold fronts can turn those small, man-made hills to ice. That said, the best thing about midwestern winter resorts is that they exist, period—it's better than not being able to snowboard at all. You can always have fun on a snowboard, and a snowboard will always make any place more fun. Indeed, the greatest thing about snowboarding in less-than-ideal Midwest conditions is that they inspire invention. Creativity rules the roost in areas with lotsa winter but little elevation: as a result, a surprising number of snowboard pros come out of these smaller, local, not-in-any-official-guidebook kinda places. On ice, you can work up some major speed, especially in the pipe.

As such, tricks and jibbing form the fun at places like this: bereft of champagne powder, hardcore midwestern snowboarders teach themselves how to ride anything, from sliding handrails in the town square to hucking homemade jumps in the backyard. Using one's ingenuity to make fun on a snowboard is the essence of riding here: that snowboarding remains so vital in such places shows that you really can snowboard anywhere. The reason? In the Midwest and places like it, people ride because they love it—because they want to more than anything in the world.

Riding Europe

Even looking at the terrain in continental Europe in photographs makes clear our friends across the Atlantic enjoy some of the best snowboarding ever. Mountain ranges like the Alps epitomize the ideal snow-sport destination. Yes, Europe is Mecca for mountain riders. 'Boarding there, I really feel like I'm wallowing in the primordial ooze of snow-sport history: they call 'em "Alpine" sports for a reason. And the sheer beauty on display continues to stagger me, from the impossibly jagged, immense peaks of the Alps to the Pyrenees' gorgeously shaped slopes to the Italian Dolomites, a mountain range with unique red hues and beguiling primitive rock formations.

The great thing about Europe is that every winter-sport area is so close, you can move around at will. Many separate resorts are connected by runs, and sometimes you can ride the slopes from one country to another in one day. But it's nice to take your time, too. When I first taught my friend Robert how to snowboard back in 1999, we traveled across the Alps over twelve glorious summertime days.

We started in France, riding the glacier at Tignes, happy to discover five inches of fresh powder waiting for us. We spent a number of days there until we moved to Switzerland's Zermatt at the bottom of the Matterhorn, where we again found fresh snow for the taking. At the top, it's steep enough to make good turns, but there are also long groomers to practice going straight and fast on. On the way up to Le Petit Matterhorn, we had to wait for the wind to stop throwing our cable car around until we could land; it was a great way to get the adrenalin pumping, I'll tell you that.

Then we headed towards Austria's Pitztal valley, near where they once found a five-thousand-year-old man in a glacier. We arrived in Mayrhofen, encountering a storm that lasted two days. That was our summertime tour. You can snowboard all summer long throughout Western Europe if you so desire: it's a beautiful way to learn.

By the end of the '99 winter season, Robert was heliboarding! Part of his snowboarding success was due to his own skills and determination, but the experience of riding all that inspiring, varied European terrain I believe cranked up his skill level. After riding through the best that France, Switzerland, and Austria could offer, Robert was ready to ride anything.

SWITZERLAND: RIDING THE "FUR COAT CAPITAL"

Switzerland features some of the Alps' most glamorous snow resorts like Gstaad, St. Moritz, and Zermatt, but the glitter belies this teensy country's incredible terrain—the most mountainous in all of Europe. And everything is all so clean, wonderfully clean. Welcome to Switzerland.

Davos

At over 5,000 feet, Davos—the site of the 1928 winter Olympic games—is the highest town in Europe. It's a sophisticated place, too, where many diplomats come to meet.

St. Moritz

St. Moritz is best known as an exclusive place for rich and infamous Eurotrash; the great website boardtheworld.com calls it the "fur coat capital of the world." It's easy to see why St. Moritz attracts the beautiful people—just the journey to get there is beautiful in itself. Runs here are groomed to perfection: no expense is spared to make sure conditions are ideal. The Swiss are incredible ecoconservationists, so everything is deliciously clean and green. *That's* Switzerland.

AUSTRIA: SAUERKRAUT AND SNOWBOARDING

My favorite thing about Austria, besides the powder, is that you can get sauerkraut while snowboarding; 'kraut is served at every restaurant on the slopes. In Austria, I also had maybe the second-greatest steak I've ever eaten, a perfect chateaubriand which paled only next to the T-bones at Buck's T-4 in Big Sky, Montana. Oh, the snowboarding's pretty good, too—*massive* understatement there.

Austria is a primeval snow-sport region, down to its fairytale Alpine villages that are right out of a Christmas special. The vibe is very old-world European: there's a sense of history permeating Austria that one doesn't find many places. Great resorts like Kitzbuehl, Lech, and St. Anton deserve their prestige, but great experiences are possible almost anywhere there's snow.

St. Johann im Pongau

St. Johann is mainly for vacationing Austrians—I barely heard English when I was there. And even though it's not as well known or elaborate as other more famous Austrian destinations, the mountains are still among the most epic and gorgeous I've ever seen. Riding in St. Johann, I realized I'd received greater immersion into another culture than I might have if I'd hit the more well-known resorts.

ITALY: BRAVO SNOWBOARDING!

I like the Italians. Period. It's a pleasure to go to Italy for any reason; if I happen to go there for snowboarding, well, what a great combination. Whenever I return from Italy, I always make sure my backpack's stuffed with a gallon jug of the most sublime olive oil I've ever tasted. The only thing I don't like is having to give up my passport in Italian hotels (it's the law, alas).

Italy's winter resorts and mountains are absolutely, unbelievably beautiful, and the food is fantastic. Some of my favorite snowboard spots are clustered throughout the Aosta Valley, on the south side of Mont Blanc, Euope's highest mountain, which casts a thrillingly imposing Alpine shadow. Heli-boarding in Valgrisenche, riding on and off-piste in Cervinia on the Italian side of the Matterhorn—it's all great, with stunning scenery that doesn't look like anywhere else . . . although you might recognize some of Italy's mountain ranges from old "spaghetti western" movies, which often substituted these landscapes for the American West. In a word—epic.

Another big plus with riding in Italy: you can heli-board there, unlike France next door, where helicopters can pick you up, but not drop you off. My favorite thing to do is start in France, snowboard into Italy, then get a helicopter to take you back up to the top of the mountain and ride back to France.

Cervinia

One of the best snowboarding areas in Italy, and therefore the world. Once I was snowboarding Cervinia in the springtime: as I rode, I'd hear loud crashing noises. When I looked across at the mountains in the distance, I saw huge snow-slides crashing down. Beautiful, rugged, fierce, Cervinia's on such a massive scale, it inspires awe.

Alagna

Near Alagna lies Italy's Monte Rosa *massif*, the second highest peak in all of Europe. To get there, I drove up an endless valley that rambled on forever. When I finally arrived, however, I found myself surrounded by pristine mountains, the perfect likes of which I encounter all too rarely.

Courmayeur

This resort area is cherished for its mellow, elegant slopes in the shadow of Mont Blanc—perfect for beginners, but in a setting that's uniquely old-world charming. And you're in *Italy* . . .

FRANCE: VIVE LE SNOWBOARDING!

Outside of the United States, France just might be the second largest center of snowboarding in the world. Why? Because there's so much of France that you can ride. And then it's just so . . . *French*. Another good thing about France: you eat like the French. In France, I eat *foie gras*, or maybe the local myrtle berry pie. I drink regional white wine at lunch—er, when I do drink at lunch. My favorite meal ever I experienced at a restaurant called L'Etoiles de Neige in St. Martin de Belleville: calf liver, and of course the local cheese plate that comes after the main course but before dessert.

Another favorite meal of mine took place high in the French Alps near Megeve, at a restaurant that only could be reached by helicopter. That was my first heli-boarding experience, and the moment I learned everything was possible while riding. Depending on where you go, you can snowboard all year round in France: I've had great snowboard experiences on Tignes' Grand Motte glacier during summer, and seen Olympic ski teams practicing there as late as August. To paraphrase *Scarface*, the world is yours here—your snowboard is merely the passport.

You feel that you own the world every time you go off-piste in France. I've gone so far off-piste there, I've found myself in the middle of nowhere high in the Alps, where the only way back is to call for the heli to come and get you.

Chamonix

Possibly the mountaineering capital of the world, with challenging terrain so rugged you must hire a guide—or two. Encompassing Europe's largest peak, Mont Blanc, Chamonix is more than just another "ski area": its dramatic landscape looks like the place where God will eventually go to retire. The snowboarding reflects the mountaineering culture; everything in Chamonix is geared towards riding *all* of the mountain—heaven for a freerider like myself.

Groomed runs seem boring compared to Chamonix's natural pleasures. Here, I take the lift to farthest reaches, then go off-piste, snowboarding in the opposite direction of the resort until I can go no further. There's nothing better than a bluebird day surrounded by the sharp, jagged rocks of Chamonix's graphic black-and-white peaks. Chamonix's Michelin-starred Albert 1er restaurant is equally sublime: its *Savoie* tasting menu is incredible, each course centered on local delicacies like freshwater fish, paired perfectly with a different local wine for each dish.

Chamonix is most famous, though, for the infamous Vallée Blanche, the longest ski run in Europe, if not the world, spanning nearly fourteen miles. Surprisingly, it's not that intimidating: the Vallée Blanche isn't too steep for the most part, but you'll need to hire a local guide to ensure a safe descent and avoid dangerous crevasses.

Les Trois Vallées:

Not a resort per se but three valleys that comprise many resorts with epic results, the most famous being Courchevel, Meribel, and Val Thorens. In the Vallées, I often find myself surrounded by untouched powder as far as the eye can see—in all directions. Over the course of a day riding here, you see no buildings save the odd mountain shack no one has lived in for a hundred years. At the same time, Courchevel is *ritzy*: On a sunny afternoon stop for lunch on the deck at Chalet Pierre to see a real scene: it's like "fashion week" all winter long. Chalet Pierre's great innovation: strolling musicians in cowboy hats serenade you with Texas music at the top of the French Alps! *C'est unique, bien sur* . . .

But Courchevel's main attraction is that it has the most amazing, varied terrain—you've got the option of doing everything from most extreme backcountry to easy runs. This is extreme territory made for extreme fun: coming down the side of the mountain I'd find natural powder half-pipes, gullies that made for nice jumps, and any number of couloirs to get crazy in. Any type of jump or trick you could ever dream of was possible here in Mother Nature's elite terrain park. And Les Trois Vallées offers the largest ski expanse connected by lifts—they brag about it. That's life at the top, snowboarding in France. Everywhere you go, you're a million miles from anywhere.

The Outer Limits: Snowboarding Off the Beaten Path

Traveling the world on a snowboard, I've seen some of the most glorious sights in all of Europe and the United States. But what's surprised me most is how much of the world I've seen via snowboarding that I never thought I'd experience. Traveling to these places has broadened my world view—I now watch the news differently, with a more trained, knowing eye.

In my youth, we were fed so much propaganda during the Cold War. However, snowboarding in Eastern Europe later in life gave me a perspective about the complexity of the actual situation. Right now, the Islamic world is the center of much global controversy, but I got to see for myself how a venerable African-Muslim culture really lives (and has for centuries) when I rode in Morocco.

Mountains + snowboard = the *lingua franca* I speak when I find myself in these unexpected realms. Through them, I see how the world is both different and the same everywhere. Of course, it's not different for those who live in such places—snow provides a shared way of life wherever you find it, the glue of unity for a near-universal Alpine sensibility.

RIDING AUSTRALIA: SNOW AND VEGEMITE

In fact, the first time I lived outside North America for any significant amount of time was when I went to teach snowboarding in Australia at Mount Buller, a resort area just four hours north of Melbourne (it's three if you're Australian). Talk about culture shock: the national foodstuff is vegemite, a bitter, concentrated yeast-extract spread. "Ever since World War II Australian troops have depended on Vegemite for a taste of home," claims vegemite.com.

Snowboarding in Australia is its own thing, too. In Australia, they have barriers right in the middle of runs—they're nets to catch out-of-control skiers. They need them; it's a necessity in out-of-control Australia. I also loved seeing "wombat crossing" signs along the road, and the country's various restaurants built to resemble large tropical fruits. Welcome to Australia, mate . . .

The grounded intensity of Australia's indigenous Aboriginal people and culture I'll never forget, either. They are what made me realize Australia really *is* different: whether you're snowboarding or not, it feels like the edge of the world. If you're going snowboarding, take a raincoat and a dry set of undies; It can be foggy and rainy, but it can be good, too. Don't expect Colorado conditions, that's for sure—as a snowboarding destination, well, Australia is fantastic for snorkeling. The truth is, the best thing about Australia is the passion the Australians have for riding snow. They don't have the best mountains, but they love it so much that a lot of good snowboarders ultimately come out of Australia.

OFF-PISTE IN EASTERN EUROPE

Snowboarding in Eastern Europe was another kind of story. I ended up in Slovenia with a family I was teaching—we were chasing a storm, trying to land wherever the powder was around Europe. We had been in France, but a big snowstorm had missed us completely, heading instead to Switzerland and Austria. We drove from Meribel into Italy, trying to anticipate where the storm would land.

It landed in Slovenia, and so did we. But the resort in Slovenia had been shut down and was nonoperational. Determined to get some runs, we drove high into the mountains; there were no other vehicles around. We hiked up into the mountain, and the driver went to the other side of the mountain, where we'd snowboard down later to meet him.

It was really fun. Because this Slovenian resort had been closed for years, wildlife had taken over in pleasingly anarchic fashion: trees at least fifteen years old were growing in the middle of every run. That's snowboarding after socialism for you!

SNOWBOARDING THE SOUTHERN HEMISPHERE

Whatever you do, try to have a snowboarding experience in the Southern Hemisphere, where mountain life is truly like nowhere else. That's because life there is lived in the shadow of the Andes mountains, maybe the most spectacular ranges after the Himalayas; in fact, in size the Andes are second only to the Himalayas. The Andes are so long, it's said their expanse could stretch from Los Angeles to London.

That's the scale you're riding inside in South America. One of my favorite riding experiences occurred in Chile, and I fantasize about going back all the time. In fact, Chile's where the seeds of this very book were first planted. The Chilean people are also stunningly beautiful, kind, and hospitable in every way. And Chile's not just about snowboarding: there's a lot of other culture there to soak up, too. Don't miss the iconoclastic love poet Pablo Neruda's wonderfully surreal residence-museum when you're in Santiago.

In Chile, I rode at Portillo in the shadow of the Andes. Portillo is definitely one of my favorite resorts. For one, a big, shaggy St. Bernard just chills out in the lobby, greeting visitors. Portillo's both incredibly remote and utterly sophisticated.

Portillo's 123 rooms are perched on the precipice of the mountain pass that connects Chile with Argentina, on an epic mountain lake; we'd awake every morning to see the Chilean army doing military exercises on the lake's frozen surface. At the amazing dinners in the resort's comfy restaurant, where the courses never seem to end, super-courteous waiters would ask if you wanted bottled water or "water of the lake," which is what came out of the faucet. You always want the water of the lake: it's the freshest water you've ever drunk—think bottled water on tap.

I found the size of the mountains around Portillo astonishing—19,000-foot peaks constantly remind you of the Andes' record-setting status. There was so much space on Portillo's runs, and with absolute zero daytrippers I felt totally alone on the slopes. I often was; I *owned* the mountain. And there was some of the best, most plentiful snow I'd ever seen. I was there for two weeks near the end of the season, and we must've had *at least* four fresh-powder days. And that's in the height of North America's summer—*August* is their midwinter season!

Before I got there, ten meters of snow had already dropped. In fact, I arrived in a blizzard—the first day was a whiteout. Then we had to leave a day early because a storm was coming and if the pass got snowed in, we'd have missed our plane.

We should've stayed in Chile just a *little* longer, I think, and waited for the snow to melt. However, I would say probably my most exotic and magical snowboarding experience happened when I got the chance to ride in Morocco.

MOROCCO: THE UNTAMED MOUNTAIN

My Moroccan snowboarding adventure started when we flew into Marrakesh to spend the night. The next morning, our group of five included Jean-Paul Grassot, an expert French high-mountain guide. No matter where you are in the world, if you have a French high-mountain guide, you're in good shape. Ultra-trained and certified, French high-mountain guides wear their uniform proudly whenever they're on the slopes. Everyone feels safer alongside a French high-mountain guide. I felt utterly comfortable in Jean-Paul's unflappable hands; he never sleeps, planning, calculating, making sure everything is ideal all the time in the most unpredictable of places.

The other guide was a local Berber, decked out as well in the French guide's uniform. We worked out of the base of Mount Toubkal, where the French have built a huge rock building as refuge. The Moroccan food was great, too—various cous-cous options, or lamb cooked Bedouin style. It wasn't the usual reheated chili that you find at so many American winter-resort restaurants, that's for sure.

We drove up the mountain to the end of the road, where a Berber village lay. There, we packed our gear onto donkeys, and some local guides took off with our stuff; we then walked all the way up. Miles and miles we hiked. We spent four days going up and down: we'd wake up in the morning, put on our skins and crampons, and amble vertically for six hours. At the peak, you're so in the boonies. You might even have to walk up *another* mountain to get back to base.

The riding was amazing in Morocco—at the top, we were completely isolated. It was a distinctive sight: from snow-capped peaks, we'd look out onto the desert.

In Morocco, you're mountaineering as much as snowboarding. There was no such thing as a helicopter rescue up high in the Atlas Mountains. If you wreck yourself up on the mountain, it's up to Allah to save you. In avalanche conditions, you want to be out with people who know what they're doing down to a science. It's like choosing hunting partners—you don't want to go with someone who doesn't know how to shoot a gun if you're trying to take down a six-point elk. In Morocco, the French Mountain Guides served as our gun, the mountain our elk.

Eventually our posse ended up in Tchediyat, the highest Berber village in Morocco. The year I visited, the town had just gotten electricity. Tchediyat's female population dressed all in very bright-colored clothes; when you'd look into the fields, you'd see little orange and red dots—women tending the sheep.

In high Atlas villages like Tchediyat, you will hear the Muslim call to prayer at the same times every day. Instead of the loudspeakers now used in Marrakesh, they have a live person doing the prayer from a high tower, just like in olden days. I knew I was in a different place when I heard that call at sunset on a remote, snow-capped African peak.

"Snowboarding in Africa"—even though I've done it, the phrase still sounds funny coming off my tongue. Never, ever in my life did I think I was going to snowboard in Africa. It wasn't even an aspiration, but it turned out to be a great idea. I experienced Morocco from the top down—it's a great way to do it.

The Ultimate Journey: Life from the Top Down

"Many is the child who journeys this high to be different," Bear Claw observes in *Jeremiah Johnson*, "planning to get from the mountain something that nature couldn't get them below . . ." Per Bear Claw, as soon as I experienced mountain living, I knew I was different like that. The reason I became a snowboarder, in fact, was because I wanted to see the whole world from the top down: it's the best view. The point is, you can have fun anywhere on a snowboard. When you're a snowboarder, you take your pow where you find it, whether it's up in high-stakes Morocco, or in the tall glades at the Skyline Skiway in small-town North Dakota.

Snowboarding is all about options. About movement. About *journeys*. About riding successfully through literal peaks and valleys. You'll make it. On a snowboard, you can truly go anywhere. I know—my life's the proof.

I can be standing on a cliff during the summertime, and my fear of heights will resurface. But on same cliff on a snowboard I no longer fear heights. It's because I'm in control on my snowboard. I want to be there on that cliff, looking as far as I can toward the horizon. They don't call it the "top of the world" for nothing. And remember—it's better to ride the top without falling . . .

The Physics—
and Metaphysics—Behind
No-Fall Snowboarding

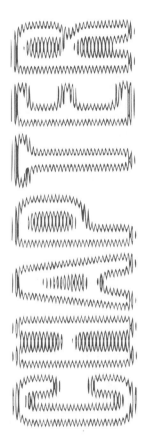

"A motorcycle functions entirely in accordance with the laws of reason, and a study of the art of motorcycle maintenance is really a miniature study of the art of rationality itself."

—*Robert M. Pirsig,* Zen and the Art of Motorcycle Maintenance

've been developing my no-fall technique for ten years on my own, and always felt I was doing something right. I've talked earlier about "felt physics"; in other words, I knew my technique worked because it *felt right.* It *worked,* and that was enough for me.

However, as I began work on this book, I realized I wanted to test my no-fall technique against hard science. I didn't want to instruct people to use my technique without knowing for sure the science behind it was utterly sound. To that end, I contacted David Lind.

I would say *Dr.* David Lind, but when I met him he asked me not to use "doctor" in his name—he's that kind of humble, unpretentious guy. I'll stick with "professor," which is apt. More than anything, Professor Lind wants to teach and express his knowledge. His modesty belies his genius, while his credentials speak for themselves.

After receiving a Ph.D. in physics from the University of Washington, Lind went on to start the nuclear physics program at the University of Colorado at Boulder. Professor Lind is also an expert, if not *the* expert, in the physics of snow and avalanches. In particular, he is a specialist on snow sports: in 1996 he published (with co-author Scott P. Sanders) *The Physics of Skiing: Skiing at the Triple Point*, the authoritative text on the science behind skiing and snowboarding.

What impressed me beyond Professor Lind's obvious expertise in the subject was his passion. Now eighty-six years old, Lind has been skiing since 1930: at the age of twelve, he made himself a pair of skis out of a couple hickory planks to ride his local Snoqualmie Pass in Washington State's Cascade mountain range. I know I talk a lot of smack about skiers, but more than anything I respect Lind because he's the consummate mountaineer: since his hickory-plank ski days, he's skied or climbed mountains wherever his studies took him, from Europe and Japan to India.

Indeed, Professor Lind knows the mountain inside and out both from experience and theory. He knows what it *feels like* to ride a fresh-powder day or skid down ice, and what the physical, scientific rationales are behind those experiences. I knew that if I asked Professor Lind to put my technique to the test, he would tell the truth—explaining not only *why* my technique worked in scientific terms, but also whether or not it was the most effective and efficient way to snowboard.

In particular, I wanted to compare the "official" way I'd been taught and accredited to teach with the no-fall method I've developed myself. I wanted to put my technique truly on the line. If it didn't work, if it wasn't the most refined and perfect it could be according to the laws of physics, I wanted to know before I wasted *your* time.

Let's just say my highest expectations were confirmed. And then some.

The Physics

I met Professor Lind in the Duane Physical Laboratories building one August afternoon on the picturesque campus of the University of Colorado at Boulder, where he is currently professor emeritus. Professor Lind took us up to the top of the building, the highest point on the entire campus, where I was to demonstrate my technique.

I'd brought with me an old Burton Rippey pro-model snowboard with 2003 Burton C16 bindings attached, as well as my patented practice board—a device I designed specifically to practice my no-fall snowboarding movements on, which I'm hoping will be commercially manufactured and distributed soon. "Compared with the several virtual-reality snowboarding training gizmos already on the market, [Martin's] device seems extremely simple," *The New York Times* wrote of my practice board.

Professor Lind took one look at my practice board and immediately understood its function. While Professor Lind had never snowboarded himself, he was fully aware of every aspect of a snowboard's technical details, from varying cambers to how sidecut affects the ability to turn.

First I went through my entire technique for Professor Lind: I explained the Neutral Balanced Position, how to steer with the shoulders, and why I use one's natural-stride distance to determine stance. Right away he got what I was trying to accomplish. "The entire philosophy of your technique is that it develops the forces applied to the edge of the board via internal forces, rather than by having to change the center of mass position relative to the board," he noted.

For comparison's sake, I then showed him the "official" way to snowboard that I had been accredited to teach by the American Association of Snowboard Instructors: this method involves the twisting of the lower body—hips, knees, ankles, feet—to steer and balance the board.

A smile crossed Lind's face. "In the conventional method of snowboarding, when the board goes forward, it has to drag the mass," he told me. Alas, such dragging is inherently unstable and will most likely drag you to the ground: in conventional snowboarding, the board controls you more than you control it. Worst of all, according to Lind conventional snowboarding relies on the body twisting to effect turns. "To have the most control on a snowboard, you want to control the tilt and angulation of the board without exerting a lateral force so that it twists," Professor Lind explained. "In the conventional method, however, you are exerting that twisting lateral force. If I move my hip, that's going to put lateral pressure on the board, which you don't want. Your method keeps the center of mass neutral, leaving the center of mass at rest as much as possible. It's advantageous to *not* move the center of mass relative to the snowboard."

Conventional snowboarding, Lind explains, relies on the rider having to "rock the body" to turn. "When the snowboarder stops that rotation, it creates an opposite torque in the lower body, which tends to turn the rider in the wrong direction for the maneuver they're trying to make." In my no-fall technique, Lind notes, the rider applies the necessary forces to the snowboard, but *without* exerting those other, destabilizing forces simultaneously.

Lind was saying that what made my no-fall snowboarding technique succeed was that it followed a maxim of basic physics that almost anyone could understand: every action creates an equal and opposite reaction. When, as my no-fall method suggests, the snowboarder raises the shoulder to turn, it creates *an equal and opposite reaction* in the lower body. In this case the reaction occurs in the foot, causing either the heel or toe to compensate and push the snowboard edge into the snow and cause a turn. "What you're doing is enhancing the steering action of the edge when you load your weight onto the front foot, which is causing that edge to turn," Professor Lind clarified.

"The board is inherently a part of you," he continued. "The body is a structure: in your technique, when you lower your shoulder, that's automatically going to raise the foot on the same side. Because of the inertia of the shoulder, there has to be an equal and opposite force that pulls the lower part of the body. In your method, you're creating an articulation between the lower and upper body."

I asked him what that meant in layman's terms. Professor Lind smiled anew. "With your method, you don't have to spill so much," he responded.

"You don't have to spill so much." The words echoed in my brain. At this point, barely fifteen minutes into the meeting, Professor Lind confirmed a decade's worth of my work: that with my snowboarding method, you

will fall less and be more balanced than the way it's taught at resorts around the world. "The essential point of your technique," Lind explained, "is you're keeping the center of mass moving stably."

So neutral isn't so bad after all, is it? Heartened, I asked Professor Lind if, other than improved stability, there were other advantages to no-fall snowboarding. "In your method, you can implement reactions much faster," he said. "To rotate shoulders back and forth, as you're suggesting, is not as drastic as trying to push mass from one side to the other, as in conventional snowboarding. You're letting the snowboard generate the necessary force to move. If one steers a snowboard with the lower body, as is traditional, you have to exert a torque strong enough to get the center of mass back up—that takes a long time, and it's not as accurate."

In order to react quickly, Lind explained, one part of the body has to work against another part to set up the geometry right. "Your technique allows for much faster reaction," he said. "Moving the shoulders is not nearly as drastic as actually trying to push the body's center of mass from one side to the other."

"In your method, because you're exerting an equal and opposite force onto another part of an articulated structure, it allows you to move quicker and anticipate the feel of change," Professor Lind continued. He likened the snowboarder who properly utilizes my no-fall technique to a gyroscope's ability to stay balanced. "At speed, the snowboarder has to react in a matter of ten feet or so—he's got something on the order of a *quarter of a second* to get everything done." And, he added, with the no-fall technique, the rider can anticipate bumps, changes in terrain, or even another snowboarder faster. "You're connecting the simplest visual signal to the simplest motion," Lind said.

Professor Lind had brought up something I hadn't thought of, at least consciously: both my students and I had experienced these quicker, more instantaneous reactions while riding the no-fall method. If my technique allows the rider to "anticipate the feel of change" more quickly, that means no-fall snowboarding allows for enhanced, improved terrain reading. That alone makes for a safer day on the hill. As well, beginner snowboarders will begin to improve their terrain reading right from the start.

After an hour or so, we had thoroughly discussed the implications, in terms of physics, of my shoulder steering and NBP. However, I wanted to know in particular about the science of stability when it came to choosing a snowboard stance.

I demonstrated how I determine stance width in no-fall snowboarding: by figuring out one's individual natural-stride distance—one you normally use when you walk Professor Lind brightened. "That's an interesting point," he responded. "By determining the stance using the rider's natural stride, you're adapting the balance learned from walking to riding. The musculature then matches the geometry. I think it is more stable to be in the natural stride while snowboarding."

If my no-fall technique allows for better stability, control, and reaction response, why had the conventional, accepted snowboarding style taken hold in the first place? "Conventional snowboarding is based on the easiest, most straightforward mechanical movements that the body can make," he replied. "Your technique takes a little bit of training to sink in: the body needs to get used to it and realize the consequences of the particular movements you're suggesting." *This* I already knew.

In what seemed like no time, Professor Lind had answered my every question, and it was time to leave. As our informal seminar ended, I packed up my equipment, thanked him for his time and went on my way.

As I moved through the building to the exit, I tried to keep from jumping up and down in ecstasy—finally, all my years of work had been validated by the most objective expert I could find. Now I knew my technique wasn't just some gimmick, but an upright citizen of the universe, obeying and utilizing all physical laws to a "T." "Why hadn't I thought of doing this years before?" I wondered as I stuffed the gear I'd brought into my 1992 Cadillac Sedan De Ville.

But something else weighed on me even harder. Why hadn't conventional snowboarding instruction evaluated its methods against hard science in this way before? If they had, I wouldn't have had to write this book in the first place. No matter. Talking to Professor Lind clarified one thing to me above all: the no-fall snowboarding revolution had arrived, and science was its riding partner.

Snowboarding and the Mind

To me, Bruce Lee always seemed like the most right-brain kinda guy around. And I mean that as a compliment.

The reason I say that is, see, Bruce Lee was more than anything a *big-picture* guy. Watching him fight, you'd see Bruce sussing out the entire scenario facing him, along with all the possible attacks and counterattacks his enemies had at their disposal—all in a matter of seconds. Then he'd just start kicking some *ass*. "When you just ease the burden of your mind, you just do it," Bruce Lee once said. "That is the most important thing: how can I, in the process of learning to use my body, understand myself?"

WHEN THE RIGHT BRAIN RULES

"When someone is working in right-brain mode, it means that person has integrated the details of everything they've learned," Dr. Roger Callahan explains regarding Lee's complete focus. "They've mastered the details, so they no longer have to worry about them. Like, when someone drives a car after many years of driving, they don't think about the details of how to drive—they just go ahead and *drive*."

According to Dr. Callahan, there are many easily identified advantages to right-brain thinking. "Many great artists happen to be left-handed and right-brain dominant," he says. "Even many left-brain dominant artists study how to better access and utilize their right-brain functions more."

Dr. Callahan explains further that winter sports like snowboarding innately thrust the participant into right-brain dominant mode. "If you are coming down the slopes and going very fast, that is a right-brain activity," Dr. Callahan says. "It happens to anyone engaged in any such complex activity. As you start integrating everything around you, you become right-brain dominant at that moment. You are reading the terrain without thinking about what you're doing. You're responding automatically—having mastered the procedures, you may even do some subconscious learning. You may even *improve* on previous learning."

For Dr. Callahan, the athlete trained to fully utilize his or her right brain will find tasks "intrinsically pleasurable." "The right-brain dominant athlete is somebody who's in the position to really enjoy their sport, whereas the person still mastering the details isn't having as much fun," he clarifies.

I know from left and right brain distinctions myself. Being both dyslexic and left-handed, I've spent my whole life marinating in my brain's right hemisphere. Left-handedness and dyslexia are often indicators that a person uses right-brain functions far more than his or her left brain. For us lefties, the right brain usually serves as our anchor, for better or worse. Mostly for better, as I eventually came to understand.

It was tough for me at first, though, as most of the world runs on left-brain time. My whole life I've been told I wasn't keeping up, or, more typically, that I wasn't concentrating on the correct things.

When I found snowboarding, however, I finally found an activity that perfectly suited, even encouraged, my right-brain inclination. I began to figure out being Mr. Right Brain was maybe a good thing after all.

I first got a true sense of the advantages of consciously applied right-brain thinking during my senior year of college. Having completed all of my business-major courses, I was free to take an art class, so I signed up for beginner's drawing. To my happy surprise, the teacher taught by showing students how to access and use right-brain functions while drawing.

I couldn't do anything *but* use my right-brain functions while drawing, or just doing anything, putting me at a distinct advantage in the class. At that point, I knew I was home free: this was the first time my dyslexia ever gave me an academic advantage. I ended up getting an "A" in the class; my professor even sent my drawings on a nationwide museum tour of "right brain" enhanced art.

The textbook for this class was *Drawing on the Right Side of the Brain* by Dr. Betty Edwards, which went on to become a best seller, moving over two and half million copies and translated into numerous languages. Dr. Edwards's teachings influenced me profoundly. Finally, I thought, here's someone who understands what I've been going through. I was struck by Dr. Edwards's ideas for teaching drawing, which were based on the landmark findings of psychobiologist Dr. Roger B. Sperry on human-brain hemisphere functions.

It was in 1968, as Edwards notes in her introduction, that Sperry first presented his groundbreaking research that would eventually garner him a Nobel prize. Edwards was taken with Sperry's "pioneering insight into the dual nature of human thinking—verbal, analytic thinking mainly located in the left hemisphere, and visual, perceptual thinking mainly located in the right hemisphere."

In particular, Dr. Sperry's findings led Edwards to figure out which particular brain hemisphere was better suited, or conversely less helpful, to the act of art making. "The left hemisphere is very conservative," Dr. Edwards says today. "The right brain is good at imagining, whereas the left is very logical. They aren't always suited to work together."

One thing that struck me as *simpatico* thinking between myself and Dr. Edwards: she postulates that anyone can learn to draw if they learn the right way, in the right sequence—just as I think anyone can learn to snowboard without falling by precisely following my no-fall method's steps.

Also, Edwards's research suggested that drawing, or anything else that puts you on the right side of the brain, allows you to see the world more completely. She notes that everyone from nurses and sports coaches to psychologists, writers, hair stylists, and even private investigators has benefited from her methods of consciously utilizing the right brain. So why not snowboarding? I knew from practice that snowboarding's enhanced right-brain activity did the same thing—and if you can see the world more completely while snowboarding, the world is a safer place.

BUILDING CONFIDENCE WITH SMALL STEPS

Back in the day, encountering Edwards's philosophy of right-brain inclusiveness seriously influenced me in creating no-fall snowboarding. I wanted a fail-safe technique that was similarly specific—where everybody gets taught the same sequence of steps that leads to better all-around riding. A technique that not only anybody could learn, but one that would result in safer, more efficient snowboarding: riding that was both more fun in general and required less effort, less strain. I wished to open up snowboarders to ride as high-performance as their progression allowed.

Similarly, Edwards—who holds a doctorate in art, education, and the psychology of perception from the University of California at Los Angeles and is professor emeritus of art at California State University in Long Beach—realized a major element in a student's success in learning drawing was acquiring confidence. Dr. Edwards realized that the best method of teaching drawing would introduce just a few key skills that could be mastered easily and sequentially. Once mastered, each subsequent fundamental would enlarge upon the previous, building confidence with each successive, successful lesson.

This kind of thinking influenced how I designed the instruction presented in this book: I broke down the no-fall technique into a few key basic movements that could be learned and mastered gradually at home, *before* snowboarding for the first time. Getting the technique down before you hit the hill increases confidence, and subsequently performance, when you're actually on the hill. "The trick is in the mastery," Dr. Edwards agreed when I interviewed her for this book. "And I think you're on the right track: if someone wants to master the basic skills of a sport, or drawing, or whatever, they have to do it so thoroughly that they go an automatic."

This kind of instinctual right-brain thinking dovetails not surprisingly with martial-arts instruction. Psychologist Dr. Roger Callahan brings up my favorite martial artist to make his example. "In the film *Enter the Dragon*, which I've seen about fifty times, there's a scene where Bruce Lee is training someone how to fight," Dr. Callahan recalls. "Bruce tells the student, 'Don't think—*act!*' In other words, he's saying 'Get off your left brain!' But it's not so easy to do when you're a novice."

SHIFTING BETWEEN THE LEFT AND RIGHT BRAIN

For Dr. Edwards, vanquishing the dominance of left-brain thinking is the first step of no-fall snowboarding, too. "The left hemisphere doesn't want you to do things that cause a cognitive shift to the right hemisphere," she says. "It is always warning you to not do something because you might fall. It reminds you of, say, the last time you broke your leg, just to keep you in its little grip. If you can learn to snowboard without falling unnecessarily, the left brain isn't as able to convey such a strong message."

Ideally, Edwards goes on, the student will "let go to the point where he or she is no longer thinking *verbally* in terms of their skills. They're not constantly walking themselves through the process. You don't want the student to keep thinking 'Okay, now I have to raise my left shoulder to turn,' or whatever. The use of words, in fast-moving sports in particular, or drawing, or dancing, slows down responses. Words mess everything up." Edwards isn't alone in thinking this: Malcolm Gladwell in his book *Blink* discusses the scientific validity of how, in terms of cognitive processing, words really do slow things down.

I tell Dr. Edwards that when I'm snowboarding, I feel that I am fully in what she terms "R-mode," the most heightened state of right-brain dominance. It's a lucid yet fluid mindstate, ideal for moment-to-moment—even *second-to-second*—problem conquering.

" 'The zone' is what I think you're talking about," Dr. Edwards responds. "The right brain is extraordinarily powerful in the sense that it can encompass so much information all at once, simultaneously. Many basketball players talk about how often, while they are playing, they enter what is known as 'the zone.' If they fall out of 'the zone,' they discover they're not playing as well. What it means to be in 'the zone' is that the subject experiences a cognitive shift to the brain hemisphere that's most appropriate for the specific task at hand."

Her statement intrigues me: it suggests that there is a scientific rationale working to create the metaphysical, transcendent feeling I get while snowboarding at peak performance. I ask Dr. Edwards how "the zone" applies to extreme motion sports like snowboarding in particular. "You have to react without thinking in snowboarding—you can't think in words," Dr. Edwards explains. "You don't know what's coming next. It's the 'thinking about it' that screws people up, which is very funny."

Dr. Edwards starts to laugh herself. "I do a lot of corporate seminars, trying to teach businesspeople how to access right-brain function for more creative problem-solving," she says of her work counseling Fortune

500 companies like Disney, AT&T, and Apple Computers. "The corporate world is set up to wreck any possible creative problem solving."

I tell Dr. Edwards that since I began snowboarding, I feel my senses are more acute. That I am able to perceive the whole of things more. That, it seems, I am not just using my right-brain more, but fully integrating it into completing my left-brain tasks more easily. Is this a by-product of exercising my right-brain functions via snowboarding? Does snowboarding allow me to access right-brain cognition better even when I'm not snowboarding?

I wasn't surprised by Dr. Edwards's answer. "What creeps over into real life after vigorously pursuing a right-brain dominant sport like snowboarding is that you know the difference," Dr. Edwards explained. "You know when you are using one system of the brain and not the other. Now you can hopefully choose consciously to address each task with the proper brain mode."

I've found doing right-brain dominant activity can also carry over its benefits even after I stop snowboarding, enlivening more mundane tasks and allowing for better problem solving. "Even after you shift into more left-brain activities, having worked in right-brain mode enhances these new, more left-dominant activities," Dr. Callahan elucidates. "When you are using your mind and body together, and you feel that integration, it's one of the great pleasures in life—like sex. So naturally, the next thing you're going into will be more pleasurable."

But while I experienced how exercising my right-brain functions could help me, I wanted to know how to make such benefits tangible, lasting, and accessible for the students of my no-fall technique.

HOW THE LEFT BRAIN CAN HELP

I asked Dr. Edwards what was the best way to integrate the right-brain lessons into everyday life. Surprisingly, she said this was the exact moment to throw the left brain a bone or two. But how?

It's easy. By *talking*.

Edwards suggests that having students verbally analyze their snowboarding progress immediately after a riding session would allow them to access their right-brain evolutions later. "Talk about what you accomplished during the right-brain activity," Dr. Edwards suggests. "You want students to talk about the experience afterward—what it felt like. The brain's left hemisphere doesn't like to be abandoned; it needs to assert its territory and get a word in. If you let it do its verbal thing to analyze what's been happening, then it will more cooperatively drop out when you want it to."

Analyzing what you've done on a snowboard is particularly important, Dr. Edwards explains, in regard to advancing the rider's terrain-reading skills. "It's very difficult to teach terrain reading," Dr. Edwards says. "You cannot teach the '*gestalt*—it's too complicated." The *gestalt*, Edwards explains, is what happens when the students finally understand and are able to execute the necessary skills to snowboard: that's when they can start to truly comprehend the concept of "terrain." "Reading terrain happens when the students' skills are all working together," she says. "They become conscious of a kind of insight into what snowboarding *is*—the totality of it."

"The key," Dr. Edwards concludes, "is to get your snowboarding students to make the cognitive shift to the appropriate brain hemisphere *consciously*, whether they're riding or not." Snowboarding, indeed, puts you right there—on a snowboard, you don't need to do anything to give the right brain a jumpstart into lucid slow motion. "In the state when you are experiencing the *gestalt*, time seems to slow down," Dr. Edwards continues. "Or disappear."

That is what I was most excited to learn the root of—the sense of timelessness one experiences while snowboarding. What Dr. Edwards describes is the scientific basis for how good I feel when I snowboard.

"The day is long, this high," Bear Claw notes of mountain life in *Jeremiah Johnson*. And when riding the mountain, the snowboarder almost never notices the passage of time. When people talk about snowboarding and surfing having a mystical, meditational quality, however, it's not just New Age fantasy. It's something real triggered in the neurochemistry of the snowboarder's brain hemispheres, as Dr. Edwards makes clear.

It's no surprise that time becomes irrelevant when, right away, snowboarding switches the rider into a right-brain dominant mode. When I'm riding, I can only tell time by the grumbling in my stomach. I talk a lot about what I like most about snowboarding, but this time I really mean it: what I like most about riding is that, on a snowboard, you can make sure time isn't controlling *you*.

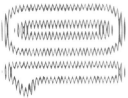

Calling All Old Dogs . . .

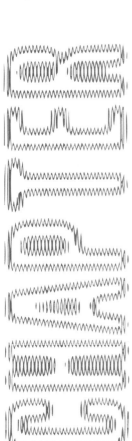

"To me, when I'm teaching, all types of knowledge ultimately means self-knowledge. . . . [My students] want to learn to express themselves through some movement. . . . What I'm saying therefore, is [the student] is paying me to show him, in combative form, the art of expressing the human body."

—Bruce Lee

Because snowboarding and its technology constantly change and improve, methods of snowboard instruction should also change to keep up. When I first started snowboarding, the board's edges had no sidecut—they were straight like an ice skate. With this primitive setup, grossly exaggerated movements were necessary just to get the snowboard to turn. With the implementation of sidecut and camber into snowboard design, today's boards now turn via even small shifts in the rider's body weight.

Over many years both teaching snowboarding and observing others teach the sport, I've noticed many different styles and ways to ride. This breadth of experience has given me the ability to see and improve inefficiencies in all kinds of teaching conventions.

In my no-fall method, for example, I purposefully avoid teaching big body movements like leaning and twisting the hips that are central to most institutionalized snowboard instruction. This doesn't mean that snowboarding cannot be done the other way; I just feel I've found the most efficient way to do it.

How to Unlearn Bad Snowboarding Habits . . .

When learning a new sport like snowboarding, maintaining a progression that consistently builds on each task helps speed up the learning process, saving time and energy for everyone involved. If you've learned to snowboard previously, or taken lessons before attempting my no-fall snowboarding technique, then you may have acquired habits your body must now unlearn in order to attain supreme board balance. Most likely, you've learned methods or skills that you'll abandon or find inadequate after exposure to no-fall snowboarding. Unless you know what not to do, these vestiges of unstable snowboarding can interfere with learning to ride using my no-fall technique. Here are a few must-avoids from the conventional snowboarding of the past:

Sideslipping

"Sideslipping" is taught in many schools of snowboarding instruction—it's typically the first thing students learn in a typical snowboard lesson, along with the fact that they're going to fall. When a beginning student is taught to side-slip, she is learning to balance on her heels while sliding straight down the fall line. This usually involves no-fall no-nos like lifting the toes, leaning back, bending at the waist, twisting the body, and placing the hands out front for balance. The unlucky snowboard neophyte will most likely learn some combination of these movements as a means to ride.

It is *possible* to ride using these balancing movements; it's just not the most stable or efficient approach available compared to no-fall snowboarding. The conventional methods of learning to snowboard are fine for students who have no problem with constantly falling down and picking themselves up throughout their lessons.

Compare teaching snowboarding with, say, teaching someone how to drive a car. You don't need to continually crash your car and run it into ditches in order to develop driving skills. You definitely don't need well-intentioned, if misled, instructors rewarding such collisions, telling you "Good job—try it again!" as they pick your battered body off the ground.

One of the first things most learn in conventional snowboard instruction is how to stand up and slide down the hill on your heels. This is called a *heel-side sideslip.* In the process of learning this, you will most likely have to stand up and sit down many times. This will happen because (surprise!) you haven't yet developed the balancing skills to stay upright. Learning this sideslip maneuver first is not only difficult without the proper balancing skills: you are also learning how to make the snowboard function in the exact *opposite* way that it is designed for.

After you develop into an adequate snowboarder via my no-fall technique, however, you never have to sideslip again.

"Pet the Dog" and Other Dead-End Snowboarding Gimmicks

Most snowboard instructors mean well, and try to communicate their ideas of how to ride in the most accessible language they can. This often results in not just unstable technique, however, but unintended hilarity.

On your first day learning to snowboard conventionally, you may be asked to snowboard via the infamous "pet the dog" method, or the "I'm a little teapot" technique (an Australian non-innovation). Maybe even you'll be asked sometime to perform my favorite, "reach for the door knob."

Your snowboard instructor will ask you to mimic these movements and positions familiar from real life on the board, but they don't have much to do with actual snowboarding. If you try to "pet the dog" on a snowboard, you'll actually be throwing your mass out of balance; to counter, you'll have to throw in an awkward, twisting countermove that'll just destabilize you further. In reality, "petting the dog," being "a little teapot" and "reaching for the door knob" are all arbitrary variations on how to catch edges on your first day on a snowboard.

Achieving your first turns on a board will also prove more difficult with these madcap methods. When you reach across your snowboard to "grab the door knob," or reach down to "pet the dog," point your hand like "a little teapot" in the direction you hope to move in, you are steering your snowboard with your hips, unintentionally driving your downhill edge into the snow in the process.

Foot Steering into Oblivion

Beginners using such inefficient balance methods are also taught to steer with the feet in combination with the hip-steering required by "pet the dog" *et al.* Foot steering uses up a lot of unnecessary energy and is difficult to learn. In the beginning, the slightest slipup or miscalculation of these moves will typically end up with your edge catching in the snow and you falling down on either your butt, hands, knees, or elbows.

This emphasis on teaching foot steering perplexes me. Why would anyone teach a beginner such inefficient, difficult moves on their first day learning to ride? On the other hand, I've designed my no-fall technique so that the basic balancing movements are easy and clear enough to be learned very quickly.

Most of my students manage to master basic balance on the first day. The novice boarder can then move more smoothly from this initial point to riding more aggressive terrain and conditions. With my no-fall approach, beginner snowboarders know right away that if they find themselves bent, twisted, unbalanced or out of control, they'll be able to return to the alignment of the NBP and prevent themselves from falling.

This is what my students who first learned snowboarding the conventional way appreciate more than anything: that, if they feel themselves going out of balance for whatever reason, then the steps to get back in the groove are clear. If you ride the no-fall method correctly, soon you'll discover that being in anything but perfect balance feels unnatural and unstable.

But to each his own: if you enjoy falling while snowboarding, it's your prerogative—stick to the old school. Just make sure you don't run into me while you're tumbling down the mountain . . .

A Note to
Fellow Snowboard Instructors

The biggest myth about learning snowboarding is this: the first-timer must spend three days falling before really absorbing how to ride. Anyone who attempts to learn to ride with this attitude deserves respect just for the effort, as this approach isn't easy.

TEACHING NO-FALL SNOWBOARDING MOST EFFECTIVELY

Say you're leading a group of ten first-time snowboarders—what's the best way to help them? I mean *all* of them. The first one or two people who are able to get down the hill on their own, it's easy to tell them "Good job—do more of that!" The instructor inevitably spends more time on the students who progress more slowly, neglecting the faster students. The class keeps pace with the slowest student.

A group lesson like this is a frustrating dynamic: the instructor wants to help everybody. However, the slower students tend to receive instruction of greater depth than the faster students.

After enough trial and error and cheering, most snowboard students can figure out how to fall less just in the interest of self-preservation—forcing oneself to figure out some way, any way to balance a little better assures a slightly safer trip down the hill. Then again, the nascent snowboarder doesn't really need an instructor to do this, anyway. If you put any number of people up on a hill and tell them to snowboard down, 10 percent of them will figure out how to do it in some fashion regardless of whether there's an instructor there shouting "Good job!" or not.

In the span of a one-day snowboard lesson, most students experience a wide range of emotions, in no particular order: confusion, frustration, relaxation, stress, success, elation. They might direct these feelings toward themselves, toward the instructor, or toward snowboarding itself. Maybe they're fixated on a problem that they should've left at home; any kind of mental block can hold back a student from progressing.

In the beginning, the student might be scared, or just plain *stiff*. As students warm up, however, they tend to move with more flexibility. However, they will reach a state of fatigue quicker then they expected; when students get tired, that's when accidents start happening. The instructor has to monitor each student's fatigue level throughout the whole day. You don't want to have to drag your students down the mountain at the end of the day—you want them to take that last run on their own steam.

I've learned that my job as an instructor is to help my students refine the way they move. If you enable them to move their bodies in a smooth, refined, and proper sequence while on a snowboard, then they will better sustain their balance and control, all while having a great time.

If you teach your students proper balance techniques, maybe they won't get just one real run down a hill—they might progress even further. Many times I've found my beginner students acquiring enough skills on that infamous first day to experience a few different types of terrain and conditions by the end.

The most important quality necessary to learn snowboarding, however, is best shared by both teacher and student: *patience.* For the instructor, not becoming frustrated by your student's seeming inability to get it is crucial: everyone has different aptitudes for learning. And even if students are learning the clearest, most accessible and stable snowboarding technique, they're still going to experience developmental stumbling blocks along the way according to their own individual makeup. After all, the movements they're expected to learn are initially unfamiliar compared to those they make off the mountain during everyday life.

Hopefully, the no-fall road map provides a clear enough path for all to follow; you just have to get your students' bodies to go along with their minds. Through enough repetition, the movements will become instinctual, and the student can really start to ride without worrying excessively about the details.

Ultimately, my method has been designed to make both teaching easier for the instructor and learning more accessible to the student. The no-fall technique provides students with the necessary building blocks: if you let them build it, "it" will come.

Conclusion

There are three basic themes that play out in the typical tragicomedy of learning to snowboard: the snowboarder vs. himself or herself; the snowboarder vs. skier-dominated society; and the snowboarder vs. snowboarding itself.

When the "snowboarder vs. himself" scenario is in play, the thing that keeps you from learning to snowboard is the fear that you create yourself. As Winston Churchill once said, "People stumble over the truth frequently, but most just pick themselves up and carry on as if nothing happened." For some, snowboarding presents a self-fulfilling prophecy—your left brain says you could never successfully do something so . . . *extreme.* You'll surely fall; you'll most likely hurt yourself, no question. Why even try? Why take a second lesson?

In the "snowboarder vs. skier-dominated society" theme, the snowboarder is taught how to snowboard through the prism of skiing. The student is to think of and ride the snowboard as a single ski. As a result, this potential rider never is able to ride the snowboard correctly *as a snowboard.* If you aren't riding the equipment right, you can't ride to the fullest of your potential. Falling is never entirely out of the question in this instance; full balance is never achieved.

In the final theme, "snowboarder vs. snowboarding," snowboarders reveal how stuck in their ways they are. Sometimes, even when presented with a better option, the snowboarder refuses to change; she has "always ridden like this." Some snowboarders fear that if they change their mode of riding, they'll lose their precious "individual style," even if that style ends up blowing out their knees.

Even if something a snowboarder does is wrong, if it's lodged in habit, it might stay there forever. Snowboarders started as rebels, remember? What rebel likes being told what to do? At the same time, snowboarders—including myself sometimes—are strangely far more susceptible to trends and fashion than most. As a snowboarder, one can find oneself either stuck in the mud, or blowing in the winds of change way too freely.

Each of these situations stems from the one fundamental question: what is *real* snowboarding? There's a million answers to that question, all coming from factions within factions. The freeriders say that all-mountain riding is the true path—that in riding the mountain to the fullest one finds snowboarding's real soul. Freestylers, meanwhile, think that individual expression on a snowboard is best expressed through tricks—jibbing, the half-pipe, jumps, grabs.

If I'm trying to say anything in this book, it's that all of the above is true. With my technique, the idea is that you can do it all, and better, and more safely. If you want to ride the whole mountain, no-fall snowboarding gives you that access. With my technique, eventually you'll be able to ride any kind of run, in any conditions. The technique allows you to adapt and adjust to ride anything.

If you're into doing tricks and jumps, my no-fall method adapts to that mode as well. With my technique, you'll ride your tricks in the pipe or park more smoothly. It's a paradox: the more stable you are, the more extreme you can ride.

Maybe you have no interest in being a serious freerider or freestyler. Maybe you just want to ride groomed trails and have an easygoing good time on the mountain, just cruising perfect runs and carving to your heart's content. I hear that. However you want to snowboard, you can do it no-fall style. Over all applications, the principle remains the same: you're riding more balanced, and therefore riding to your fullest potential.

"Balanced" is the most positive adjective one can use to describe something. Think of the satisfaction you get when your checkbook is finally "balanced." When the "balance" of colors in your living room finally comes together. When the "balance" between self-fulfillment and making big money aligns itself in the most unexpected way.

My concept of balance, as you know now, derives from the martial arts. It's the balance that allows you to react faster, to do more. It's the balance that keeps you from falling. Others have explored the parallels between martial arts and snowboarding, and used what they've learned to their advantage. Iconic "soul rider" Craig Kelly never lost sight of the spiritual aspect of snowboarding; it's no coincidence that he was a devoted student of t'ai chi and yoga—you could see it in his riding.

The key word, of course, is support; one can't have balance without support. And yet, there are different ways snowboarding can provide support. A friend of mine told me about how he went to Whistler in the midst of a terrible divorce. He found he didn't have to obsess about his romantic problems when he was going down the mountain. Or, rather, he couldn't. If he thought about anything other than reading the terrain in front of him, he wouldn't have a successful run. He just did it.

Snowboarding provided not just a break from his routine, but simply the act of snowboarding itself helped "empty his cup" of unnecessary baggage: after that trip, he was finally able to see his failed relationship for what it really was. Spending a week alone using his right brain to solve snowboarding's moment-to-moment issues opened him up. After that week in Whistler, he found himself more able to approach his relationship problems perceptually, giving them more big-picture analysis.

You see, there's not a lot of daydreaming on a snowboard. Snowboarding keeps both mind *and* body active. Daydreaming is the petri dish of paranoia, where you imagine the various scenarios about the problems in your life mushrooming out of control.

"What is my life going to be like if she leaves me?" is a typical refrain of the garden-variety paranoia we all encounter at some point. "What is going to happen if I don't get that bonus?" You know, it's the stuff of classic country and western music: if she leaves you, are you going to be eating dogfood for dinner and drinking beer for breakfast?

You don't think about that stuff while snowboarding. You can't. Or you just won't get down the mountain. Now, when you hit the après-ski bar and someone puts on a sad old Johnny Cash song and you start knocking back Stella Artois, those thoughts might start popping up again. But at least those hours you spent snowboarding gave you a respite, allowing your head to clear for a while.

Harrison Ford said once to interviewer Charlie Rose something to the effect that, when you're piloting a plane, it's the greatest combination of focus and relaxation. You're so focused on keeping the plane in the air (and on the safety of you and your passengers) that the menial aspects of life that take up so much of the day seem righteously unimportant. In fact, you don't think about them at all. Once you're back on land, this experience stays with you—now you can put all the b.s. into perspective much more easily. That's been my experience flying "Snowboard Air."

In time, snowboarding becomes nothing so much as a transcendental state balancing both meditative calm and knife-edge lucidity. Snowboarding remains an addictive paradox—strenuous physical exercise that promotes balance in both body and soul, yet still allows the rider to thrash out in the pipe and get *extreme*. I hope you've felt something similar as you've followed the lessons of this book—and continue to feel it as you progress as a snowboarder.

It's funny: I had an epiphany when I was interviewing Dr. Betty Edwards about how snowboarding works with right-brain functions. That moment of enlightenment actually came up after the interview was done. Dr. Edwards had been talking about the biggest struggle of her career: getting politicians—and even educators themselves—to stop stripping art education from our nation's school curriculums. While the establishment regarded art as "extra," she felt kids needed to learn to see just as much as read. She talked about how kids are assaulted with images that they have to decipher all the time—that the word "image," in fact, is the root of "imagination."

Discussing the struggles in Dr. Edwards's educational field made me think about the struggles in mine. I'm a snowboarding instructor; this is what I do, just as my father was an accountant and that defined his life to a certain degree. As a snowboard instructor, I have to teach. But I found myself teaching in an environment that didn't prize what I love about teaching or riding.

"You are going to fall" was the message I kept hearing; I couldn't accept that. "Only twelve, *maybe* fifteen percent of your students will return": so goes the industry mantra. As a professional who wants to make money, there was no way I was accepting that. And as the humanitarian I consider myself to be, I just couldn't see people hurting themselves and not enjoying this strange sport I'd devoted my life to. This book is my way of clearing the air. It's my way of emptying the cup.

Indeed, it's my way, period. In fact, there are many ways to snowboard: I just think mine is the best. The point is, now you, the snowboarding consumer, have a choice.

Since the early days of Hawaii's existence, surfing was a holy privilege. Only Hawaii's *ali'i* warrior royals—the descendents of the gods—were allowed to surf. Then resident missionaries banned the practice, and for many decades no one could surf in Hawaii. Thankfully, this isn't the case with snowboarding today: now, everyone can be a snowboarding god. More than anything, I want people interested in snowboarding to have the most options possible—options about how and what they learn to ride.

Now, not only can anyone snowboard, but they can do it without falling. If you've been following the instruction in this book fairly religiously, then you're the living proof of this. And I'm guessing things are looking up—chances are you'll just keep progressing, and progressing, and progressing more if you keep following my instructions. On the other hand, the deliciously cruel beauty of learning to snowboard is that, no matter how good you get, there's always going to be something else new to experience.

A new mountain, untried terrain, a run steeper than you've ever attempted, a country farther away than you've ever traveled—snowboarding keeps sending new phenomena your way to challenge you and keep you on your toes. The mountain will always be bigger than you: it sounds hokey, but it's time-proven winter wisdom. At least now you have the tools to rise to the occasion the mountain provides. So what are you waiting for? After all, the world is yours, remember?

Now ride it.

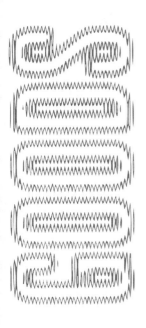

An Opinionated List of Everything You'll Ever Need to Go Snowboarding

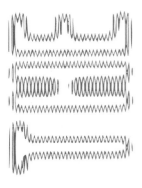

Next to learning how to snowboard correctly, the gear you use to ride with is what affects your snowboarding progress the most. Snowboarding is a highly technical sport, and your equipment is your direct conduit to the snow. With the right gear, you can snowboard better, longer, and safer.

The following is an opinionated list, from outerwear to boots to energy bars, comprising everything that someone would need to go snowboarding. It reflects the gear that I myself use; I figure if it's good enough for me, it's good enough for you.

A hard truth to learn about snowboarding: you always want to ride the best possible equipment, which often means the most expensive equipment. There are cheaper options—it is possible to buy boards, for example, for $150 or less—but typically you get what you pay for.

Like many snowboarders, I'm a gear head—I obsess over my gear, constantly maintaining and refreshing it. I feel most comfortable using the best, most up-to-date, snowboard-specific gear possible.

I typically ride at least two hundred days on the mountain every year: between my personal riding and years of teaching, I've road-tested and researched tons of gear, so I know what works. Throughout my career, I've always tried to be as knowledgeable about snowboard equipment as possible. For years, I was typically the only snowboard instructor to attend nearly every sales presentation that snowboard companies would make for the staff of The Other Side, Beaver Creek's famous "core" snowboard shop.

Attendance at these sales presentations was required for Other Side employees, but I just did it in my quest to learn everything I could about snowboarding. I suffered through many a boring marketing lecture, but I'm glad: now I can tell you exactly what to buy to make sure you're snowboarding with the best gear possible, customized to your individual needs.

I mention a lot of Burton products in this section of the book. This is not because Burton sponsors me, nor do they give me any free stuff (although I do receive a pro discount thanks to my instructor status). But I find that Burton typically makes the best gear overall, year after year. This has something to do with the amount of money Burton allocates to the research and development of new and better snowboard products.

Burton is one of the first-ever snowboard companies and helped develop the sport of snowboarding—all they make is snowboard-specific stuff. And as Burton accounts for nearly one-third of all snowboard sales, they have resources to sink into research that smaller companies can't always match.

As well, while many famous ski companies make snowboards, I like supporting a company that is solely in the snowboard business. Buyer beware: there are many snowboard brands out there that spend most of their money on marketing, not product, and just want your money. If you go for cheap, you'll most likely be riding junk.

Necessary Snowboard Clothing

Clothing is indisputably important to snowboarding. Snowboard-specific clothing is highly technical, designed for the sport's particular needs. The best snowboard clothing is as waterproof, windproof, breathable, and rugged as possible. When it comes to dressing for snowboarding, think layers: weather conditions change all the time, so you want to be free to adapt. Remember, if you're not warm and cozy in your snowboard clothes, your riding can suffer. Make wise choices in the clothing department, however, and you'll be fine.

1. Thermal Underwear: For colder-weather conditions, make sure you've got some kind of good long underwear, some quality wool long johns and shirt; I like to rock the classic union suit. As you'll be sweating and getting covered in snow, look for good quality moisture absorption, too. I like wool because it keeps you warm even when it gets wet. Many companies like Burton also offer more technical, sport-specific options featuring high-tech, breathable fabrics, many of which will wick sweat away to keep you both dry and warm as you exert yourself.

2. Snowboarding Socks: Your snowboard boots should fit snugly over just one pair of socks. Burton "boneout" snowboard socks are my favorite, and here's why: they have more fabric in the places that you need it, less in the places that you don't. Because your feet are in boots that strap to a binding, you'll be putting stress on your feet from different directions. A good snowboard sock is thinner over the bridge of your foot where it gets the most pressure; therefore, it won't fall, bunch or get loose at the toe and make your feet uncomfortable. For colder conditions, try to have a heavier, wool-based option. Remember, the boots themselves are very well insulated.

3. Headgear: Headgear is important for warmth and head protection. Your body loses much of its heat from the top of your head, so keeping it covered when you're going to be outdoors during winter conditions is essential. I recommend carrying a wool cap to allow for easier regulation of your body temperature; they seem to come in handy all the time, especially for those moments on the hill when you need to take off your helmet. Snowboarding helmets also keep your head warm, but most important they provide crucial protection. Riding with a helmet is a must, especially for beginning boarders. All helmets are not created equal. Sometimes cheaper helmets offer better protection than more expensive options; sometimes vice versa. Do your research; there can be huge variations even within the same brand of helmet. Also, stay sport-specific with your head protection: bike or skateboard helmets may not provide the right impact resistance for snowboarding. I recommend checking out the latest reviews in *Consumer Reports* to find the best snowboard helmet available—that's what I do.

4. Snowboard-Specific Outerwear: When it comes to outerwear, I prefer Burton's AK Continuum series. That's because the AK stuff is the ultimate when it comes to water resistance, breathable fabric, pocket options, and vents. Other things to look for are a good hood and powder skirt (an elastic band that goes around the waist that prevents snow from creeping under your jacket). My snowboard outerwear philosophy follows the layer system. It usually consists of just a shell, albeit a high-tech one designed to keep wind out and me totally dry. Under that I add layers of fleece, shirts, and sweaters depending on conditions. A great snowboarding jacket should also have good ventilation, like zips under the arms to let heat out when you get too warm. As well, on the hill your jacket serves largely as your backpack, so check out the pocket storage, too. Such highly technical features and innovations end up costing extra *dinero*, but staying comfortable on the mountain makes it more than worth it.

5. Neck Gaiter: When you are out in the elements all day, you need something to protect your face and neck from wind, sun and cold. A "neck gaiter"—a fleece tube that covers the neck—should do the trick. You can pull the gaiter up to cover the lower half of your face in extreme cold, or wear a full head-and-neck covering "balaclava" ski mask, complete with eye and mouth cut outs. In either instance, you may be mistaken for a bank robber or a ninja, so only bust the balaclava out when necessary.

6. Vest/Fleece Layers: I have a heavy Burton AK goose-down vest that I wear as a layer when it gets really cold, and a lighter version when it's not. I like a vest to have a few pockets for extra storage capacity, too. For icier days, having an additional long-sleeved fleece zip-up can make the difference in ultimate on-hill comfort.

7. Snowboard Trousers: When snowboarding, you're going to be on your butt *a lot*, either on snow, ice, or cold-metal chairlifts. Therefore, your choice of snowboarding trouser is crucial—they must truly resist the elements. Look for the most water-resistant, breathable fabric you can find; good pockets, side vents for air circulation, and fleece lining in the seat are pluses you'll come to appreciate as well. The higher-end Burton stuff is what I ride. Generally, the better and more technical (i.e., warmer and more waterproof) the trouser, the more expensive. But it's money well spent. Oh yeah, your snowboard trousers should be comfortable, and look cool, too.

8. Snowboard Gloves: Over a day of riding, you'll discover your hands go in the snow often. Because the feet are locked together in the bindings, us snowboarders tend to sit on the snow to rest between riding sessions. To stand back up, you're going to use your hands to push up off the snow. Therefore, having good-quality gloves is essential for keeping your hands dry—you can't have a glove that soaks up moisture readily. You may like to have an extra replacement glove liner or two to go along with the outer shell; if one pair gets wet, it's nice to have a backup. Look for quality gloves using high-tech, breathable, water-repellent fabrics like Gore-Tex. If you're going to ride in warmer weather, you'll want lighter-weight gloves that breathe and keep you dry.

9. Wrist Guards: Wrist guards are a must when snowboarding, especially for beginners. Try to find as snowboard-specific a wrist guard as you can.

Some gloves come with wrist guards built in, but they're often not as effective as others. Burton, on the other hand, sells a wrist guard that was developed with input from a doctor—that's the kind of attention to detail you want in wrist protection.

10. Eye Protection: Goggles and sunglasses offer both warmth for the face and eye protection. It's always good to have at least two choices of eye protection when snowboarding, if not more. I carry one pair of sunglasses and two types of goggles when I'm riding. If one pair gets fogged or damaged, I always have a spare ready. There are so many different kinds of lenses available, all designed for specific conditions. When boarding, for example, I'll carry a lemon-yellow Oakley "fog lens" goggle and then a darker, mirrored "sun lens" pair for bright sun. Many also like amber-colored lenses, which are designed for all-around conditions. Oakley goggles are very technical—they design the shape of the lens to mimic the curvature of the eye itself to minimize optical distortion. As well, be sure to have a dry "defogging" cloth with you on the slopes to clean up wet or fogged eyewear.

11. Snowboard Boots: Boots can make or break a day of snowboarding. At the beginning of each season, I try on as many snowboard boots as I can before I make my choice of which ones I will wear that winter. Boots are a very important part of the snowboarding ensemble—if not *the* most. There are many different kinds of snowboard boots for different kinds of riding, with varying fit and stiffness. I often like Burton and Northwave boots—both of which, not coincidentally, are made in Italy and reflect that country's tradition of footwear quality. Regardless of brand, when I buy snowboard boots, they must meet three specific criteria:

A. Fit: They must hold my heel down solidly in the heel cup. This ensures there's no missed communication between me and the snowboard. Even the slightest lift in the heel of your boot can reduce your control while snowboarding.

B. Warmth: The boots will keep my feet warm and comfortable. When I say warm, I mean *toasty*; when I say comfortable, I mean they're soft but a good fit, with no sharp ridges or pressure points. I also like a boot to be flexible at the ankle bend; if your boot is too stiff in the ankle, you'll have a reduced range of motion, limiting your maneuverability.

C. Style: The boots must look good! I do not want to walk around looking like Frankenstein with big, stiff, bulky-looking devices of torture on my feet. I want stylish devices of torture on my feet. My advice: go to the store and try on *every single boot* in your size until you find something suitable.

Essential Snowboard Hardgoods

1. Snowboard: When choosing a snowboard, you want one that suits your height, weight, and foot size. Snowboard lengths are for the most part measured metrically, in centimeters. A very long snowboard, for example, would typically be around 165 centimeters or longer. Here's how to choose the right *length* for your snowboard: while you are standing, hold the snowboard up in front of you, standing it upright on its tail. Measuring up from the floor, you will want the "nose" or tip of the board to land somewhere between your chin and eyes. Nowadays boards are made to fit virtually every foot and body size. If you wish to ride a narrower snowboard that's too small for your foot, the solution is to ride with greater foot angles on the snowboard to avoid toe and heel drag. No matter what length snowboard I choose to ride, I like my stance to be centered on the sidecut. Either way, it's most important to find a snowboard that will accommodate your personal stance width. You do not want the snowboard to dictate your stance. Again, the price tag on a snowboard can often serve as a good indicator of quality—I find myself typically nabbing Burton's most expensive board, the Custom X, for example. If you can test drive a board, that's best: many board manufacturers sponsor "demo days" at mountains across the country. If you're in the market for a board, it's not a bad idea to sync up your vacation with "demo days" and actually ride the model you're interested in. One more buyer-beware caveat: you have to be really careful and do your research before you shop. Sometimes a salesperson's "enthusiasm" is influenced by the fact that if they meet a sales quota on certain equipment, they get one free themselves.

2. Bindings: The most important things to look for in bindings are stability, comfort, and response. I like to wear a softer boot with the stiffest, lightest, most responsive binding I can find, like Burton's top-of-the-line, carbon-based C60 model. On bindings, the high-back serves as a leverage device that attaches you to the snowboard via straps across the bridge of your foot. The straps are best if they are soft and comfortable, but without too much stretch. A solid fit of your boot in the binding will transfer your moves to the board more quickly and with less effort than a looser, more flexible binding.

Essential Snowboard Accessories

1. Sun Protection: Snowboarding is an outdoor, daytime sport; the reflection of the sun off the snow is very strong, so your skin will be constantly exposed to ultraviolet rays. Therefore, protection is necessary: I use Dermatone for both sunscreen and weather protection when riding. Just remember: don't forget your sun protection—you don't want to miss a day on the slopes due to a bad sunburn or sunstroke.

2. Tools: Keeping a compact set of tools on hand can defuse any number of snowboarding technical surprises. A screwdriver is key if you need to change binding angles or repair or replace equipment; a file or sharpening stone always proves handy for on-hill edge sharpening.

3. Hydration: You've got to keep your hydration up while heavily exerting yourself on a snowboard. It's not just the workout that can dry you out, but also the combination of high altitude and cold. The solution? Wear a water bladder on your back ("Camelbak" is a good brand) or just keep a water bottle in your pocket. It will save you! Keeping hydrated plays a big part in your ability to balance: your body functions better when you maintain a consistent and appropriate amount of H_2O.

4. Sustenance: To carry some type of energy bar or quick snack while riding is smart. If there ever is a time that you need a boost of energy, it will most likely happen during an intense snowboarding workout. Trust me— it's hard to balance on an empty stomach.

5. Safety Gear: Alongside helmets and wristguards, many riders utilize additional safety equipment to ride with greater confidence. Knee pads and elbow pads are not uncommon, while tailbone-shielding butt pads are very popular—although as you master no-fall snowboarding's movements, hopefully you'll find less and less need for butt pads. As much as possible, try to buy safety gear that's made specifically for snowboarding.

6. Tuning: Tuning your snowboard is a complicated (at least at first) technical process that requires specific equipment and materials. In particular, tuning requires a heating element such as an iron, special wax for the base, and a file. If you really want to learn to tune your board, searching any number of websites can give you the basic information, so I'm not including that here. However, another option is to have a ski or snowboard shop tune your board. Often, these shops have specific tuning equipment and skilled technicians. Also, the shop will know the current snow conditions, and what type of base waxing will work best on them. Some quick tuning tips: for powder, you want a freshly waxed board. For icy conditions, you need a special cold-weather wax; for slush, they have special warm-weather wax that helps the board slide easier over watery stuff. If it's new board, you or the shop should de-tune the tips and tails: de-tuning *unsharpens* both ends of the effective edge, allowing turns to happen more readily without catching anything. As for edge, most snowboards these days come with a bevel to the edge that is 90 degrees or sharper (I personally like the side edge at 88 degrees and the base at 1 degree). You or the shop should always make sure edges aren't dull or damaged; often, they can be repaired overnight.

Tech Specs: Why a Snowboard Does What It Does

On some level, all of us are at least a little interested in how the things around us work. Why does the golf ball behave as it does when you cut? How do the reverberations of strings turn into a guitar solo? How does House of Pies in Los Angeles get their fresh peach pie to taste so freakin' good? And why does my snowboard work the way it does?

When snowboards were first built, they were based on a great idea— riding mountains like a surfer on a big endless wave of snow. As the sport grew, enterprising companies worked to make that idea better through research and development, and the equipment began to evolve into what's available today.

Snowboards today are built with full-on recreation in mind, but you'd be surprised at the science that goes into building a board. Snowboard makers have incorporated into board design specific shapes, angles, and materials that, when manipulated correctly by the human body, can be used to your advantage.

Here, I'm going to explain how the snowboard works from a technical perspective—why the board does what it does on snow. Knowing something about the stats and specs of snowboard design comes in handy when renting, buying, or riding a snowboard.

Snowboard manufacturers never stop designing newer, better equipment. Using technologically advanced materials, snowboard companies work to increase the performance of each new model. The materials they use, and the way they combine them technically, come together to enhance the snowboard's function.

When choosing a board, make sure to pick one that functions best for your specific needs: keep in mind the type of snowboarding you plan on doing most often. Some boards are very high performance indeed, and some are not.

Some, called *freeride* boards, are built very sturdily with all the best material and technology, and are designed to handle all mountain terrain and snow conditions. Others are made of less durable, less costly materials which decrease both the weight, price, and often the quality of the snowboard. These *freestyle*-oriented snowboards may make it easier for doing trick and aerial maneuvers, but they may not be suitable for all-mountain terrain conditions.

In particular, how a snowboard rides is determined by a number of significant factors that determine the board's specific shape and construction.

OVERALL SURFACE AREA

The board's length multiplied by the width equals the board's total surface area. Depending on your own weight and size, this surface area is what you will be using to remain buoyant when snowboarding in less-stable surfaces such as deep powder.

WAIST WIDTH

The *waist width* of the snowboard is the narrowest point in the middle of the board. The narrower the board, the quicker it moves back and forth from edge to edge, enabling the rider to make quicker turns. The *length* and *width* of the snowboard work together to support the rider's weight, helping the snowboarder to float on the snow more easily. Because the board is wide and long relative to the rider's size, it displaces the rider's weight. This is how all boards work, be they short or long, wide or narrow.

The size of your foot determines the width of the snowboard you wish to ride. You want a board wide enough to ensure that you avoid *heel and toe drag*—when the heel or toe of the boot hangs over the edge of the snowboard and drags in the snow, affecting both speed and balance. You want toes and heels to be positioned directly over the appropriate edges *without* dragging.

Some riders, in order to make quicker turns, may wish to ride the narrowest snowboard possible. If the length of your foot is greater than the waist width of the board, you'll need to increase the angle that your foot rests on the board so that toes and heels don't drag.

Usually the shorter the board, the sharper, easier, and more readily it will turn. The more length and width a board has, on the other hand, the more buoyant it is. As a result, boards specifically designed to ride powder snow tend to be longer and heavier; boards designed to do freestyle tricks tend to be lighter and shorter. Having a shorter snowboard in the beginner stages of learning will aid your ability to make shorter and quicker turns, as well as enabling you to better control your speed and direction.

CONTACT LENGTH AND EFFECTIVE EDGE

The *contact length*—or running length, or running surface length, as it is variously known—is described, in David Lind and Scott S. Sanders's book *The Physics of Skiing*, as being the part of the snow-riding device "that contacts the surface of the slope during normal performance."

Along the snowboard's contact length run edges designed with a very deliberate shape. Along the entire base edge of the board runs a strategically placed metal strip. This metal strip spans what's known as the board's *effective edge*: per *The Physics of Skiing*, the effective edge is defined as "the part of the edge of the snowboard that is in contact with the snow when it is engaged in a turn." These edges are honed to be very sharp—sharp enough to cut through ice and snow.

SIDECUT

Snowboard edges carry the shape of two semi-circles or crescents curving towards each other; these curves determine the shape of the snowboard's turning arc. If you look at a snowboard, you'll notice it tapers to the board's middle or center, making it narrower than its tip and tail. This shape is called the snowboard's *sidecut*.

Lind and Sanders define sidecut as "the depth of the curved edge measured at the waist of the [snowboard]." Both heel-side and toe-side turning arcs share the same curve on both the left and right sidecut; the result is that each kind of turn is a mirror image of the other.

Regardless of whether your board is on the heel or toe side, when the edge meets the snow, the rider immediately begins initiating a turn—the turn following the arc of the metal edge's curve. The rider uses this board's sharp edges by either cutting *into* the snow (*carving*) or shaving the snow (*skidding*). You are making a carved turn, for example, when the edge cuts into the snow, following the designed course of the curved edge. *The Physics of Skiing* describes the geometry of a carved turn to be "the sidecut value taken with the contact length, [which] gives the ratios of that turn."

The size of your turns depends on the relationship of your board's inherent *sidecut radius* to its contact length. The smaller the sidecut radius and the shorter the running length of the snowboard, the tighter the turn you'll be able to make. Having a snowboard with more running length and a larger sidecut radius, meanwhile, gives the rider more stability at higher rates of speed. But while larger snowboards float better in deeper snow conditions than smaller boards, remember that they take more effort to turn in general. The rule to remember, anyway, is this: the higher the sidecut radius number a board has, the larger the turns it wants to make.

CAMBER

A very important factor in how a board works is the built-in arch of the snowboard, called *camber*. You can see this arch if you lay your snowboard base down on the floor. The tip and tail of the snowboard remain in contact with the ground, yet the waist and center of the snowboard is lifted up off the ground. This amount of lift is the *camber*. Snowboarding .com defines camber as "the amount of space beneath the center of a snowboard when it lies on a flat surface and its weight rests on the tip and tail." In *The Physics of Skiing*, camber is defined as "the curvature of the [snowboard's] running surface when it is under no load."

When you are snowboarding down a slope you are standing on the camber's curvature, forcing it flat. That flattening causes the running surface to then come in full contact with the snow and engage your "effective edge." According to *The Physics of Skiing*, camber works to "[increase] the [snowboard's] stability by controlling the boot load, which is transferred through the [snowboard] along its length to the tip and tail." Camber gives "life" to a snowboard. Notice how, if you stand fully strapped in on a snowboard, there is a spring or bounce to it, almost like a trampoline; that's camber.

The amount of camber defines a snowboard's responsiveness. Because of the spring camber provides, you are able to increase and decrease the pressure of your snowboard to the snow. Energy is added by allowing the camber pressure to build up as you ride through a turn; this energy is released by simply bending your knees and ankles slightly, which serves to release the pressure. If you extend your knees and ankle into the turn, you are pushing into the camber.

If pressure or force is placed on this arch, it will try to spring back to its original shape. Knowing how to utilize your board's spring or "life" to your best advantage during a turn will greatly benefit and enhance overall riding.

THE BASE

The *base* of the snowboard is the bottom of the board: it's the part that is, other than the edges, in direct contact with the snow. Bases provide a sliding surface: they're designed to reduce friction as much as possible while withstanding the constant demands on them.

Most bases are made of a polyethylene material called "P-Tex," a material designed for maximum snow slideability. A less expensive base, and the slowest, would be an *extruded* base. The more technical and costly option, the *sintered* base, can achieve greater speeds and holds wax better. "Sintered bases are much higher in molecular weight; with increasing molecular weight, abrasion resistance and wax absorption is increased," writes Missy Allemang at www.vpas.fnet.co.uk. *Graphite* is the fastest, most technical, and most expensive type snowboard base, however.

All bases are designed to be maintained with hot wax—literally by impregnating the base with wax. After scraping most of the wax off, the base is then polished into the ultimate sliding surface. It can be waxed and tuned in preparation for any specific snow condition. Snowboard bases are designed for continual maintenance and repair. Even if the base is gouged or defaced in any way, from a small scratch to a "core shot" (when a portion of the base is entirely scraped away, exposing the core), the damage can be fairly easily and inexpensively repaired, either by you or by technicians at a snowboard shop.

CORE CONSTRUCTION

The *core* of a snowboard typically comprises a combination of elements: wood, carbon fiber, rubber, fiberglass, aluminum, foam. Wood is known for its natural snap; companies like Burton and Palmer have also introduced lighter, high-tech aluminum-honeycomb cores that promise enhanced performance. Foam is considered the cheapest, least durable and most unresponsive of all core materials.

There are three kinds of core construction, the most basic being *cap* construction. About.com defines a cap board as one using "a manufacturing technique where the topsheet comes all the way down to the metal edge on the side of the snowboard." A cap just goes over the top, in other words; cap construction is typically the cheaper, easier way to manufacture a board.

Then there's *sidewall*, or *sandwich*, construction, which About.com defines as one where "a sidewall or strip of metal is used along the side of the snowboard in between the topsheet and the edge." The additional, reinforcing sidewall often provides more response than a cap board. Hybrids between cap and sandwich boards are also popular: a board might incorporate some level of both sidewall and cap construction at the same time. On some level, all current boards are "sandwich" boards, made up of many different layers and elements.

The kind of core a snowboard has is as variable as the many different companies making them; each brand has its own combination of materials. How snowboard manufacturers choose to put all these materials together to achieve camber, sidecut and the overall shape of the snowboard evolves constantly with each new innovation.

Everybody has their own idea about what kind of construction is better. Personally, I hate cap boards: to me, every one I've ever ridden has felt less responsive. A sandwich-construction board functions better for me all around; it feels more stable under my feet. In my experience the more expensive the board's inner materials are, the better it rides. But that's just my opinion.

BINDINGS

Bindings are the devices that hold you onto the snowboard. Bindings that utilize *high-backs* are most common. The high-back is the part of the binding that rises up along the back of your lower leg. A snowboarder uses the leverage that the high-back provides to move the board at an angle to the snow. The more pressure applied to the high-back, the more the snowboard increases its angle to the snow.

The angle that the high-back is adjusted to is called *forward lean*. The forward-lean angle determines how aggressively you'll stand when strapped into the bindings. The more forward the lean, the more aggressive the bend in your knees and ankles. The more aggressive your stance, the more you will be able to adjust the angle of the snowboard to the snow, and the quicker and more aggressively your snowboard will respond. Adjusting the forward lean to the maximum will prepare you to use your equipment to its utmost design.

Danny Martin's Opinionated Glossary of Common Snowboarding Terms

(Along with a Few He Just Made Up for the Hell of It)

> "Now, you must remember that the enemy has only images and illusions, behind which he hides his *true* motives."
>
> —*Sensei to Bruce Lee,*
> Enter the Dragon

The American Association of Snowboard Instructors: The governing association responsible for certifying professional snowboard instructors in the United States. Often abbreviated as "AASI."

Base: The bottom of the snowboard, the part that slides in contact with the snow. Most bases are made of a polyethylene material called P-Tex. Such material, when waxed correctly, slides on the snow easily.

Bindings: The liaison between your body and the snowboard. Usually made of plastic, carbon fiber, and lightweight metals, bindings attach a snowboarder's boot to the board via straps or, in the case of step-in bindings, clip-type systems. Bindings are one of the most important elements in your snowboarding gear-up.

Binding angles: The position of the binding to the toe-side edge when it is attached to the snowboard.

Bomb: A verb, as in "to bomb" ("Hey dudes, let's bomb this run!"). Bombing involves riding the board straight down the fall line flat with no turns; barring any obstructions, in "bombing" the rider can go as fast as he possibly can in a straight line on a snowboard. Bombing is popular with people who like to go really, really fast. Stopping on a dime has been abandoned once the commitment to bomb has been established— that is, unless the dime is at the bottom of the run. I love to bomb! It's not the safest way down, but it sure is fun . . .

Bogart: Verb meaning "to hold on to something most commonly shared in a devious, possessive way as if it is yours and only yours; to hoard." According to legend, this slang descended from the coolly possessive way Humphrey Bogart held his smokes in his mouth.

Bogus: *Not* cool, dude!

Camber: The built-in arc that gives a snowboard its flex.

Carved turn: When the snowboard travels across the snow in a turn, following as close to the curve of the sidecut as possible. You're carving a turn when you use the sharp side edge to cut into the snow or ice and let the turn follow through the sidecut's curved angle.

Catching edges: When the board's downhill edge digs into the snow unintentionally, causing the rider to fall very quickly (or causing the ground to come up very quickly to you). See also "Pete Rose," "Hand of God," and "Scorpion."

Core shot: Significant damage to the base of a snowboard that occurs when a rock or other hard, sharp obstacle gouges the base's P-Tex material, exposing the snowboard's core interior materials.

Downhill edge: The edge of the snowboard that is off the ground during a turn.

Duck, or "duck stance": Attaching oneself to the board with the heels closer together than the toes. As a result, toes point opposite directions, resembling the way a duck walks. "Duck" is the preferred stance of freestyle jibbers and trick riders who concentrate their efforts primarily in the terrain park and half-pipe.

Edge: The metal strip attached to the bottom of the snowboard along the sidecut. This edge is used to cut into the snow or ice, giving the snowboarder greater control over the direction and speed of their snowboard.

Effective edge: The edge of the snowboard that is in contact with the snow during any particular turn.

Fakie: Riding a snowboard tail first, in the opposite direction of the board's nose.

Fall line: The path of least resistance an object takes when gravity pulls it downhill.

Foot angles: The angle that the feet are in when attached to the snowboard. See also "binding angles."

Full range of motion: The range of distance the muscles in the body can move in, moving from full elongation to full contraction and back.

Goofy: An unfortunate term borrowed from surfing used to describe a right-foot-forward snowboarder.

Grommet: Lightly derogatory term for young brash snowboarders who push their limits to the extreme—in the process sometimes pushing other riders' patience.

Hand of God: A type of snowboarding accident that occurs immediately after you catch your heel-side edge.

Hawaii: Preferred place to live when not snowboarding.

Heel drag: When the heel of the snowboarding boot is mounted to the board in such a way that it hangs over the edge; when the snowboard is at an angle to the snow, the heel then drags on the ground. This may cause you to either slow down or lose balance.

Natural stride: The measured distance between the midpoint of each foot after taking a step. Determining snowboard stance in this way allows the rider to adapt his natural balance, the balance used in walking, to assist in the riding of a snowboard.

Off-piste: Terrain outside a resort's groomed runs.

Pete Rose: A type of snowboarding accident that occurs immediately after you catch your toe-side edge. The resulting collision resembles Pete Rose diving into first base.

Pitch: The steepness gradient of the hill you are riding. The greater the pitch, the steeper the terrain.

Reading terrain: Determining the best action to effect on a snowboard based on the rider's perception of the terrain's variegated surface.

Scorpion: A rather spectacular type of snowboarding accident where the rider falls flat on her face as the snowboard arches up, bending the spine backwards until the rider ends up knocking herself in the back of the head with the snowboard. Also see "catching edges."

Sidecut: The built-in curve inherent in the edges of a snowboard, which allows the snowboard to make integrated turns.

Sidecut Ratios: The measurement of the built-in curve compared to that of the snowboard's edges, from the nose to the board's middle.

Sideslipping: This entails riding the snowboard's heel-side or toe-side edge perpendicularly to the run's fall line, skidding across the snow to create the maximum amount of drag in order to slow down on unforgiving, steep terrain. "Falling leaf," meanwhile, means riding down the hill on the same edge, changing direction from left to right and back again across the fall line, all without switching edges.

Skating: A term borrowed from skateboarding, "skating" on a snowboard means having the front foot attached to the front binding while the unattached back foot pushes the board along on a flat surface.

Skidded turn: When the snowboard's edge travels across the snow in any other way than a carved turn. In a skidded turn, the snowboard scrapes across the snow, not following the inherent turn of the board's curved edge.

Stance width: The distance between the center of the bindings mounted on a snowboard.

Stomp pad: A rubber device that serves as a no-slip pad between the snowboard's bindings. Having a stomp pad proves advantageous when riding in any situation where the front foot is attached to the snowboard and the back foot dangles free.

Tail: The rear tip of the snowboard. When riding "fakie," the snowboarder travels down the hill tail first.

Terrain: The snow-covered variable surface the snowboarder rides.

Toe drag: When the toe of your boot is mounted to the snowboard in such a way that it hangs far enough over the edge to touch the snow when the snowboard goes up on an angle. This may cause the rider to slow down and/or lose balance.

Top, or "deck": The upside surface of the snowboard opposite the base. It's the deck where the bindings and stomp pad are mounted.

Uphill edge: The edge of the snowboard that you are standing on when you are making a turn.

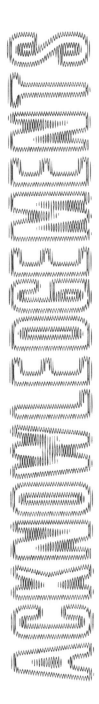

FROM DANNY MARTIN:

Many thanks to Michael Horman for putting me on the path, and showing me how great snowboarding could be, and Daniel Horman for riding with me into the future. I would also like to thank Master Holland for teaching me balance, along with many other very important lessons.

I would also like to thank Mark Seliger for helping me in every way to prepare this book—and also for being a great friend and such a powerful "free rider." I would also like to thank Ruth Levy, Matt Levy, Alex Martinegro, Kirk Edwards, Shelter Serra and everyone else at Seliger Studios.

I'm also indebted to Matt Diehl for going to all extremes on his snowboard, teaching me so much about writing and helping me put this book to bed. I can't express enough gratitude to Kim Goldstein for her interest in learning snowboarding and her powerful work with the Susan Golomb Agency in getting this book out there. I would also like to thank Doris Cooper, Sara Schapiro and Simon and Schuster for all their efforts in publishing this book.

I'm also indelibly grateful to Robert, Jenny, Rosie, Emma and William Borgerhoff Mulder for being interested in the development of my technique and their mega-support in writing this book; a special thanks to Jenny, one of the best snowboarders around, for helping me conceive the ideas for this book.

I would especially like to thank my students who rose to the challenge of snowboarding, as well as my friends who have helped me along the way: Me Sue Aloha Sue; "Wild" Bill Bain; Matt & Cloudia Bryan; Adam Schonburg; Bridget Brown; Robbie Felman; Craig and Millie McDonald; Nick Holbert; Kevin Larson; Patty, Kenny & David Raff; Robert Richardson; Ian, Eryn, Mindy & Joel Lefkowitz; Greg Ostroff; Patricio Di Tomaso; Patrick Parkhurst; Chuck Katz; R.C. Hugard; Susannah Fairley; Susan Blanchard; Tim Swanson; Cindy Delarosa; Stacy & David Rhea; Banana George; Kerry Simon; and Michael, Mike & Andrew Dolan.

I would like to thank my family for the love, support, encouragement, and prayers: Doris & Alan Martin; Ann & Don Irman; Nancy & Mark Koehn; Karen & Cary Radisewitz; John & Kathy Martin; Cliff & Kathy Scheline; Lance Fredrick; Gary Hazlett; and Reggy Souza.

I would also like to show my appreciation for those experts who agreed to be interviewed for this book: Dr. Betty Edwards [*Drawing on the Right Side of the Brain*], Dr. David Lind [*The Physics of Skiing*], and Dr. Roger J. Callahan [*Tapping the Healer Within*], and supreme fitness guru Eddie Graham. Special thanks to Vail Associates for allowing the photo shoots to take place at Beaver Creek, and to the Board Room in Avon, Colorado for all the support. Other Side and Josh Malay, R.I.P.—you will not be forgotten. Special mention must go to Teresa Riordan, Richard Chenoweth, Jennifer Scruby, and Dana Sullivan for their support, as well as Christophe Duhoux for all his mountain knowledge and great "heli" trips. And I can't forget Stephen Hill and Hearts of Space for providing the soundtrack to the writing of this book.

FOR MATT DIEHL:

I want to thank Danny Martin for his innovation and passion (and teaching me the right way to snowboard), and Mark Seliger for putting me and Danny together in the first place—and of course for his amazing photographic contributions. As well, this book would not have happened without the tireless, invaluable work of Kim Goldstein, whom really has been the glue holding this book's whole process together. I'd also like to thank our editors and associates at Simon & Schuster/Touchstone/Fireside—Doris Cooper, Lisa Considine, and Sara Schapiro—for their guidance and enthusiasm. In Mark Seliger's office, much props to Ruth Levy for holding it all together—*molto grazie*.

A big part of this book is also due to our cast of experts across a wide variety of disciplines: Dr. Roger Callahan, Dr. Betty Edwards, Dr. David Lind, and Eddie Graham. Others without whose support this book wouldn't be possible: all at the Susan Golomb Agency; Adam and Dee Dee Diehl; Alex, John, and Jonathan Fox; Doug, Lindy, Nick and Nora Blount; Greg McKnight; Todd Roberts; David Prince and Ariel Borow; Anthony Bozza; Paul Francis; Andrew, Saskia, Finn, and Aidan Moskos, and the whole Boom Chicago/Amsterdam crew; Jess Lynch and Drew Wackerling; and especially Sophia Fang.

I'd like to give a special shout-out to the editors and journalist comrades that have shaped my writing over the years, in no particular order: Alan Light, Ingrid Sischy, Jason Fine, Ray Rogers, Mark Healy, Adam Rapoport, Joe Levy, Stephen Mooallem, Scott Cohen, Nathan Brackett, Craig Marks, Sia Michel, Serena Kim, Rob Kenner, Fletcher Roberts, Evelyn McDonnell, Brad Tolinksi, Tom Beaujour, Rob Levine, Brad Goldfarb, Dimitri Ehrlich, Greg Milner, Zev Borow and Joe Wood (R.I.P.)—too many, actually, to fully list.

Lastly, this is for the late, great MyMy Diehl. Hopefully you have taken up snowboarding in heaven, where falling isn't such an issue.

FROM MARK SELIGER:

Many thanks to Alex Martinegro, Shelter Serra, Kirk Edwards, Josh Liberson, and, of course, Ruth Levy for all their help and contributions.

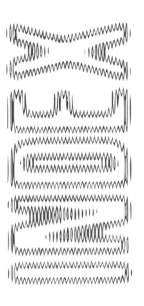